Praise for
Zero to 100,00(

"I work in digital media publishing, yet I've strugg[]
ness world, to understand how to make social med.
Jayne and Dean tackled the challenge with an energy that has to be seen to be
believed. These two are now my #1 source of information and have provided
simple and effective strategies that have helped me to monetize social media."

—**Vince Holton**, Publisher, Incisor.TV

"A fantastic, timely, and enjoyable book with serious appeal. Great work from
beginning to end. I can't recommend it enough."

—**2morrowKnight**, *Huffington Post*

"*Zero to 100,000: Social Media Tips and Tricks for Small Businesses* makes it so
easy to understand the way to successfully take your business into the 'real
world' of social media! It both entertained and educated me. I would recommend this book to my friends, business associates, and to educational institu-
tions. Brilliantly done!"

—**Debra Cincioni**, @MomsofAmerica on Twitter

"From building a bigger presence for yourself or your business, this book gets
you in on the ground floor, lays the foundation, and helps you get a jump
start on becoming a social media success. And the advice is real, not just from
Sarah-Jayne and Dean, who are awesome, but from several other success
stories they explain in the book. In a word, this book is useful."

—**Jason Falls**, CEO of Social Media Explorer and author of *No Bullshit Social
Media: The All-Business, No-Hype Guide to Social Media Marketing*

"Leveraging social media is vital for businesses of all sizes, but it is a quirky
and nuanced world where getting it wrong can have disastrous consequences.
@GrattonGirl is one of the people I see in the social space who really under-
stands the art of communicating with her audience. If you want to know how
to connect with the crowd effectively through social media, I can think of no-
one better to hold your hand on that journey than Sarah-Jayne and Dean
Gratton."

—**Kate Russell**, Technology Reporter, BBC Website and App Reviewer

Zero to 100,000

Social Media Tips and Tricks for Small Businesses

Sarah-Jayne Gratton

Dean Anthony Gratton

800 East 96th Street,
Indianapolis, Indiana 46240 USA

Zero to 100,000

The publisher offers excellent discounts on this book when ordered in quantity for bulk purchases or special sales, which may include electronic versions and/or custom covers and content particular to your business, training goals, marketing focus, and branding interests. For more information, please contact:

> U.S. Corporate and Government Sales
> (800) 382-3419
> corpsales@pearsontechgroup.com

For sales outside the United States, please contact:

> International Sales
> international@pearson.com

Visit us on the Web: informit.com/ph.

The Library of Congress cataloging-in-publication data is on file.

ISBN-13: 978-0-789-74800-3
ISBN-10: 0-789-74800-2

Text printed in the United States on recycled paper at R.R. Donnelley in Crawfordsville, Indiana.

First printing October 2011

Editor-in-Chief
Greg Wiegand

Senior Acquisitions Editor
Katherine Bull

Development Editor
Ginny Bess Munroe

Managing Editor
Kristy Hart

Project Editors
Elaine Wiley, Jess DeGabriele, and Jovana San Nicolas-Shirley

Copy Editor
Keith Cline

Indexer
Christine Karpeles

Proofreader
Language Logistics, LLC

Technical Reviewer
Karl Ribas

Publishing Coordinator
Romny French

Cover Designer
Anne Jones

Senior Compositor
Gloria Schurick

Illustrator
Dean Anthony Gratton

Dedication

For Dean and Charlotte:
Your arms my home;
Your breath my strength;
Your love the truest place.
—Sarah

For Sarah, my darling wife and best friend:
You embody my hope and my immortality.
—Dean

TABLE OF CONTENTS

About the Authors

Sarah-Jayne Gratton is an author, television presenter, and former theatre performer. She is European correspondent for the television show *You Are the Supermodel*, where she hosts a weekly segment on personal branding.

A former actress, Sarah-Jayne is an influential social media persona, speaker, and writer, regularly featured in *Social Media Today* and other publications including *In-Spire Lifestyle Magazine* (in-spirelsmagazine.co.uk) and blogcritics.org. She was nominated for a Shorty Award in social media and is one of "Twitter's Top 75 Badass Women" (bitrebels.com). She is also listed in the Top 50 of *The Sunday Times* "Social List."

Sarah-Jayne studied at Cardiff University, where she received a Bachelor of Arts in Educational Psychology and later a Doctorate in Psychology. You can find out more about Sarah-Jayne at sarahjaynegratton.com and can follow her on Twitter (@grattongirl).

Dr. Dean Anthony Gratton is a bestselling author and columnist.

Dean has worked extensively within the wireless telecommunications R&D industry and has an accomplished career in software engineering. He has enjoyed a variety of roles and responsibilities in addition to being an Editor of the Specification of the Bluetooth System: Profiles, v1.1 (the original specification). He has participated in defining the initial Bluetooth Personal Area Networking profile and was active in the Near Field Communication (NFC) technology and marketing committees. His wireless research work has been patented.

Dean has developed, architected, and led teams across several new product developments for mobile phones, DigitalTV, broadband, Femtocells, Bluetooth, Wi-Fi, ZigBee, NFC, and Private Mobile Radio.

Dean is a columnist for Incisor.TV, where he has written a number of contentious articles sharing his thoughts and challenges on industry news, opinions, and gossip. He continues to make an authoritative published and vocal presence within the wireless telecommunications industry.

Dean holds a B.Sc. (Hons.) in Psychology and a Doctorate in Telecommunications.

You can contact Dean at books@deangratton.com and follow him on Twitter (@grattonboy) to enjoy his witty shenanigans and his social media and technology-related tweets. Dean is an influential social media persona and was listed in the 50 "Top Dogs" of Twitter (bullsandbeavers.com). You can also read more about his work at deangratton.com.

Acknowledgments

We'd like to kick off our "thank yous" to Katherine Bull and Romny French, who clearly demonstrated saint-like patience during the review, copy, and editing processes. We did it! Also, a big thank you to our publicists Dan Powell and Lisa Jacobson-Brown for going all the way with the promotion of the book.

We also want to thank our contributors who feature in Part IV, "An Expert in Your Pocket," namely Jeff Bullas (jeffbullas.com), Lori McNee (lorimcnee.com), Paul Steele (baldhiker.com), Jessica Northey (fingercandymedia.com), and (last but certainly not least) Danny Devriendt (heliade.net and porternovelli.be). Thank you all for sharing your very valuable insight and know-how. We're sure that many will be inspired by your social media acumen.

A huge shout out to all our followers and fans on Twitter and Facebook, without whom this book would not be possible!

Our immense gratitude to Pedro Huyse and Rodney Holvoet at De Rotonde, Gent, Belgium, who kindly helped us maintain our mantra, "Write drunk, edit sober," but most of all, being great and very dear supportive friends; we miss you both. We were thrilled to discover that some of our best ideas occurred during happy hour. (Audio evidence is available to support this and is, of course, available upon request.)

Finally, a special shout out of love and thanks to Sarah-Jayne's soul sister, the wonderful (@movieangel) Marcella Selbach (affectionately known to Dean as Nutella).

We are truly blessed by all the love and support that has surrounded us during the writing of this book. Thank you to one and all.

Before You Begin

Whenever I visit my local bookstore, I like to adhere to what has become, over the years, a finely tuned process that I call *sipping and dipping*—that is, dipping into a subject of interest while sipping a double-shot cappuccino in the adjoining coffee bar! With my growing passion for social media, I looked forward to reading about how I could fully embrace and use it for my personal brand, but hit a stumbling block when I discovered nothing in the bookstore that covered this area of social media adoption. Sure, there were plenty of books on using social media within a large corporation, but nothing geared toward the personal (the smaller businesses and solo-preneurial brands like my own). My sipping and dipping excursions had become a source of frustration, and the seed of an idea for this book was sown.

Sarah-Jayne
(aka @grattongirl)

Dean
(aka @grattonboy)

The new language of social media has been extensively written about and often overcomplicated (in terms of technology jargon and definition). When Dean (who you'll also come to know as @grattonboy on Twitter) and myself (@grattongirl) started thinking about this book, we knew one thing for certain: We didn't want it to be one of those books! Instead, we wanted to put together an enjoyable yet educational experience that anyone could pick up and immediately find useful, regardless of previous social media knowledge.

We also wanted to take the reader on a journey through the various stages of building a successful social media presence and to do so in a way that was as engaging as social media itself. We found that there was a gaping void of social media books aimed at smaller businesses and at individuals wanting to brand themselves and their services. The prospect of filling this void fueled both our enthusiasm for the project and the passion with which it has been put together.

We hope that you find it to be a valuable and well-referenced addition to your personal library, a pocket companion along your social media journey, and a unique read to enjoy as you sip and dip your way to online success.

—Sarah-Jayne and Dean

What You Will Find in This Book

Every epic tale has a beginning, a middle, and an end; we hope that what you are about to read will translate itself into your own great social media story. It has been compiled in such a way that we hope no stone has been left unturned in terms of ease of reference and understanding.

The four sections that make up this book take you on a journey from the foundations and principles that make social media an essential promotional tool for your business to using your platforms of choice to create your own social media stage. *Zero to 100,000* takes the guesswork out of selecting the best platforms for you by providing real-life examples of how each platform individually works, along with an easy-to-use guide that will get you up and running on each of them in next to no time.

By the time you get to Part III, "The 10-Step Method to Building a Fast and Effective Online Presence," you'll already have a clear understanding of how each of the social media platforms can work to build your brand online. From there, you can journey on to discover our 10-step method to social media success with unique tips and tricks that you simply won't find anywhere else. And finally, there's Part IV, a section of one-on-one interviews with some of the most influential people in social media today—full of even more fast-track know-how to further fuel your social media fire and build upon your success.

You're Anything but Small

1

Welcome to the Big Wide Social Media Stage

Right now you're waiting in the wings, looking out toward a stage that's ready and waiting for you to step onto it and perform!

You're about to embark on a very personal journey, one that will transport your business to a new world—a world of possibility with a willing and engaged audience who are soon to become your online cheerleaders. They will advocate your brand and influence others to follow and buy-in to your products and services. Yes, it's the wonderful world of social media, and your brand is about to become its next success story.

Anyone with a little know-how can create a presence through social media, but taking that presence to the next level and making it work for your company and brand requires a little more effort. To increase visibility, connections, and revenue on a long-term basis, you need to understand your target audience, the trends that engage those within it, and the social media platforms they use. This book is all about using this knowledge to the max, and that's why it's about to become your new best friend.

More than just a companion, in fact, it'll be your personal manager, taking you by the hand and maximizing your online presence. With exclusive tips and tricks, it will help set you apart from the competition and ensure that you quickly achieve a large and loyal fan base that works to promote your brand globally around the clock.

A Shift in Worlds That Works for You

Advertising is shifting from the real to the virtual world at a frightening but exhilarating speed—a speed that opens up a world of never-before-imagined opportunity for the small business. This book shows you why it's easier than ever to compete with the big boys; you no longer have to outspend them, but instead you can outsmart them by developing viral videos, tweets, and posts that your fans will latch on to and that will blow your competitors out of the water.

Social media means outsmarting rather than outspending.

It All Starts with Personality

Your unique *brand personality* is *key* to making a successful and immediate impact. Knowing what you are "all about" in the real world is the starting point to projecting your business successfully in the virtual world of social media. So be sure you have a clear and concise mission statement that you can easily explain in 140 characters or less. We talk more about your brand personality in Chapter 2, "The Changing Social Landscape of Communication," and provide some tips to ensure that your message says all it possibly can about the strength of your brand, making its personality shine and giving it real and immediate social media oomph.

A Sneak Peek at What's to Come

But let's start by taking a look at some of the social media entrepreneurs who are featured in this book. They'll share their success secrets with you and reveal how they shaped and developed the online personas that have won them and their businesses the power to reach millions worldwide. All of them have a simple message to share, and all of them have used the advice featured within this book to turn their individual brands into online superstars.

Lori McNee

For more than 25 years, Lori McNee has lived with her family in the beautiful Rocky Mountains of central Idaho. A native of California and raised in the Southwest, Lori cultivated her interest in art and wildlife during her childhood. Today, Lori is an internationally recognized professional artist and art-marketing expert whose broad spectrum of artwork includes still life, landscape, and nature paintings.

Along with her fine arts business, Lori also juggles a professional blogging, writing, and public-speaking career. She freely shares valuable fine art advice as well as art business and social media guidance on her popular blog, FineArtTips.com. Lori ranks as one of the "Most Influential Artists" on Twitter and among "The Top 100 Most Powerful Women on Twitter." She is a television hostess for Plum TV and has been featured in magazines, books, and blogs, including *The Huffington Post*, *Los Angeles Times*, *Southwest Art Magazine*, *Wildscapes Magazine*, *American Art Collector*, *Money Dummy Blog*, *Artists Network*, *Art Bistro*, and *Art Talk Magazine*. She has been named among the "Top 10 Up and Coming Women Bloggers" and "Twitter's Top 75 Badass Women." In addition, Lori is on the Board of Advisors for *Plein Air Magazine*.

Choosing to work in a business she was passionate about was only the starting point for the success of Lori's brand. Taking the business from *dream to mainstream* came about by clever social media implementation using the tips and tricks we share with you throughout this book.

Jessica Northey

Jessica Northey describes herself as "taking over country music radio one tweet at a time." She has found a unique way of using social media to launch new artists onto radio. She shares her secrets with us later in the book, including her optimization techniques, which are now being implemented at top radio stations across the nation and in training programs that span a variety of businesses (everything, in fact, from real estate to the Walter Cronkite School of Journalism).

With a personal network of more than 160,000 followers and a second-order influence of over 4 million (more about the importance of this later in the book), Jessica is ranked in the top 500 most influential people on Twitter and, according to *Fast Company Magazine*, is one of the 150 most influential people in social media today.

Danny Devriendt

A successful blogger and an avid user of social media, Danny is one of the leading authorities on digital media and the predictive web in Europe. He is a European representative in Porter Novelli's Global Digital Council and heads up Porter Novelli's social media efforts in Europe, the Middle East, and Africa. He is based at @PNBR5, a social media lab at the very core of Porter Novelli, Brussels, from where he coordinates its cross-border digital activities.

Danny studied Educational Sciences and Agogics, the social science relating to the promotion of personal, social, and cultural welfare. His healthy passion for people, Schrödinger's cat, quantum mechanics, and *The Hitchhiker's Guide to the Galaxy* make him an unorthodox, out-of-the-box thinker.

Danny was a journalist for eight years and one of the first Belgian journalists to cover the Internet. His portfolio included several Belgian newspapers and various publications of the Roularta Media Group. He was a freelancer for the Meridian News service in the United Kingdom and was the cofounder/chief editor of *Le Grand Boulevard*, a stylish monthly news magazine. He also worked for Belgian National Radio and in local television.

A passionate presenter, Danny speaks regularly on the integrated use of digital media, web 3.0, augmented reality, predictive web, crowdsourcing and metrics, and conversation management. He has conducted media and digital media training sessions and seminars for brands and organizations all over the world. In addition, his vision for digital and social media is voiced daily through his Twitter channel, @dannydevriendt; his personal blog, www.heliade.net; and many online forums.

The Whole Social Media World's a Stage

These brief introductions hopefully encourage you to read on and discover more; after all, they are testimony to the breadth of expertise you'll find within this book. All of the featured entrepreneurs have built an exceptionally effective online presence through recognizing and promoting their individual passions and talents. They quickly learned the value of spreading their message by *word of mouse* rather than *word of mouth*. As a result of their dedication to self-promotion through social media, their success seems certain to continue to grow. They view social media as a global stage to be performed on daily and see their followers as an audience with whom they can interact and share. You need to adopt this vision, too, if you are to conquer social media and become its next big success story.

Ensure your message is spread by *word of mouse* as well as *word of mouth*, and you'll be on your way to social media success.

Perhaps the best way to paint a picture of the global media stage is to show it as a series of multilevel performance platforms. These platforms represent different aspects of social media, and each has its part to play in creating your business or brand persona.

In Part II, "Social Media Networking Basics," we introduce each of the platforms so that you can determine which is best for your brand.

Whether you decide to start with just one platform or to jump onto all of them at once, remember to take your dreams with you on the journey; allow yourself to virtually "strut your stuff" by embracing your passions and becoming an expert on the subjects that interest you most. Share and connect with others in a way that reflects your brand personality and lets it truly shine.

Your journey starts now, so fasten your seat belt and read on.

2

The Changing Social Landscape of Communication

Social media finally allows your business to be placed in the kind of global spotlight that was, until now, depend- ent on huge financial outlay. There's no denying that social media will be core to your business success, and not just for the marketing and PR departments either; it's a driving force that will affect customer services, sales, and even future recruiting.

Now for the Science Part

The whole history of business revolves around the premise of effective communication. In fact, our very language development may have come about as a need to barter or exchange with other humans. We are creative and adaptive creatures, and new ways of expressing ourselves will continue to evolve and make their way into the world we model for ourselves. Effective communication is and always will be *key* to success in life and business—it is the driving force behind many of the technological advances that continue to shape business protocols and practices.

In the fourteenth century, Ibn Khaldun, an Islamic academic, stated that he believed societies were living organisms that had cycles of birth, growth, maturity, decline, and eventually death. His was probably the first noted social science conclusion and has led to dozens of theories surrounding the science of cultural and social evolution.

Khaldun's concept of society opens our eyes to the possibilities that exist for harnessing the power of community to grow and evolve our values and ways of thinking and to sculpt the technological changes that shape our world.

If we now apply this theory to today's world of business communications, we can see that a pattern of change has emerged over the past hundred years and that new leaves on the tree of social evolution have rapidly begun to sprout. It is a cycle of change that is shaping and shifting global social enterprise. Scattered communities of knowledge, once exchanged through traditional forms of media, have united to form a global entity of communication, where everything is instantly accessible. Brand messages are evolving into condensed blocks of information that can easily be slotted into virtual outlets, and our businesses are influenced by communication in ways never before conceived.

Spread your brand message through blocks of information that can be easily shared across the many social networks.

The epitome of traditional mainstream media power was the empress herself, Oprah Winfrey. With more than 20 million viewers in tow, Oprah's community of armchair followers is loyal and believes in her *brand*. They trust her recommendations without question, and as a result, any ideas or products she features on her show or puts her name to, turn to gold. In the same way that mainstream media has given us Oprah, so today we have an amazing opportunity to create our own brand-power fueled by the driving influencers in social media and the huge communities accessible to us at the click of a mouse.

The Zuckerberg Revolution: Communication 2.0

In the 2010 article "The Zuckerberg Revolution,"[1] author Neal Gabler compares and contrasts the influence of the first printing press to the growing social media shift in communication. Gabler asserts that the press led to the concept of the *typographic man*. Of course, it makes perfect sense that as soon as communication was transposed into print, its very nature changed, leading to uniformity and a need for logical structure. In the same way, our ideas, no matter how complex, were able to be readily shared with the masses. "Print made us think better," Gabler states.

And now, here we are today, witnessing the birth and growth of the next communications revolution: social media. It is changing how we develop, interpret, and share information and has been categorized into seven principles by Mark Zuckerberg, the creator of Facebook (See Table 2.1). Coined by Zuckerberg as "Communication 2.0," it's become known as the next generation of communication.

Table 2.1   Zuckerburg's Seven Principles of Communication 2.0.

The Next Generation of Communication

Number	Principle
1	Short
2	Seamless
3	Informal
4	Immediate
5	Personal
6	Simple
7	Minimal

Gabler intimates quite harshly that this new form of communication nurtures shallowness and narcissism, and many would agree that it has robbed future generations of the ability to expand their world through the art of language. However, we can argue that this new form of communication enables the rapid sharing of information vital for personal and professional growth. It is easily absorbed and just as easily shared, making it ideal for today's fast-moving world.

We're all travelers on a new kind of two-way street—one that leads to wherever we want to go almost instantly. Our journey takes us into new territory, where the information gleaned should be used to build and market our brand personality. This is a journey of personal and professional discovery where we can rapidly adopt a huge audience of *sharers* who will, over time, use their own online influence to grow a trusted customer base for us.

1. *Los Angeles Times*, "The Zuckerberg Revolution," November 28, 2010, http://articles.latimes.com/
   2010/nov/28/opinion/la-oe-gabler-zuckerberg-20101128

Put Away the Megaphone and Put On Your Thinking Cap

That brings us to the *T* word, one that is fundamental to an effective social media presence. You'll need to achieve it to make your business all that it can be. Yes, you've guessed it: *Trust*. It's fundamental to the spending choices we, as consumers, make every day. In fact, we are very often prepared to pay a premium to have the assurance of quality that a trusted brand brings.

@grattongirl
Sarah-Jayne Gratton

Building trust is fundamental in building an effective social media presence
#socialmedia #zeroto100000 #Gratton

42 seconds ago via TweetDeck ☆ Favorite ↩ Reply 🗑 Delete

Tweets tagged with #socialmedia

There is a shift these days, however, in purchasing through personal experience and from the kind of trust that comes from the recommendation of others through online networks and groups. Purchasing is evolving, too, and has become a collaborative process. Far more people are choosing to spend based on the influence of their trusted online communities. But how does this trust become established? Do you really have to sell a huge amount of your goods and services to build trust among your followers? The surprising answer is no. What you do need to do is to become an *expert* in your field. So put away the *megaphone* and put on your *thinking cap*.

There's No One Size Fits All in Social Media

Building trust in the world of social media, or in any world come to think of it, means becoming a friend, a confidant, a problem solver, and a guide. Become all these things, and you'll gain trust; gain trust, and the sales will follow. It sounds so simple, doesn't it? And in a way it is, but it all depends on choosing and using the right social media communication platforms for you. After all, in social media, it really isn't a case of *one size fits all*, which is why this book helps you understand which particular platforms are the right ones for you.

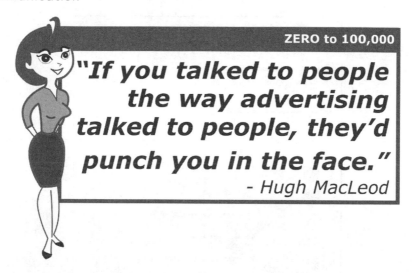

ZERO to 100,000

"If you talked to people the way advertising talked to people, they'd punch you in the face."

- Hugh MacLeod

Bear in mind that people fall in love with personalities, not with robots, publications, or PR agencies; it's a truth that you can use to both your professional and financial advantage. So when it comes to your brand personality, find out what makes it sparkle, and let it shine.

From Scattered to Unified Customer Bases

What is currently referred to as *new* media will soon become mainstream and an integral part of business operations. As we've previously mentioned, those once-scattered customer bases are now unifying through social media and are shouting their opinions across the virtual rooftops of its many platforms. As a consequence, customer feedback is *always* available—the good, the bad, and the ugly of it. And it's important to realize that even those bad and ugly comments are unlikely gifts to your brand because they provide the opportunity for your company to engage, to converse, to turn the problems into opportunities—and to dramatically amplify your brand visibility in the process.

After all, real-world surveys don't contain sections on "how much our products and services suck," so listening to our audience via social media provides us with an opportunity to glean a true reflection of how we are doing. (Figure 2-1 provides an excellent example of this.) It might seem daunting, but with this feedback your business can look forward to reaching the kinds of numbers of potential customers that your marketing budget could never have previously hoped to accomplish.

(Source: Facebook.com)

Figure 2-1   Ben & Jerry's increased sales dramatically through the customer feedback gleaned via their Facebook page.

Greater transparency is evident as we witness our networks for receiving, sharing, and amplifying information growing stronger by the day. Each individual person's ability to influence the opinions of others is becoming more powerful, allowing our businesses to feel less like passive bystanders and more like thought leaders with a real voice in the virtual world of social media.

The Power of Listening

We've talked about the opportunities that have arisen through the evolution of online communities, where influence and trust play an important part in the purchasing decision. With this in mind, it's vital to understand and harness the power of listening before engaging, instead of the other way around, and to humanly participate in discussions rather than statically broadcasting your message. Scripted answers and infomercial babble will set you back, not make you stand out, and this is where many other companies that have taken the leap into social media have got it all wrong.

But now we're scaring you! You're probably thinking that all this humanized social interaction will take up way too much of your business day. Don't worry. We teach you a method that empowers rather than impacts upon your precious time and makes every member of your staff a brand ambassador in the process.

Start thinking of yourself as a *trend explorer*. By this, we mean that you should follow the trends in your particular arena, find out what customers want by monitoring their trending topics and posts, and build a new product/service strategy in line
with real wants and needs.

In Part III of this book, we share some little-known tricks that will empower you to
shine as a true expert in your field within the social media arena. You'll learn how
to engage with key influencers to create a self-generating virtual sales force that,
over time, will provide *real* results for your brand. But first things first: it's on to
Part II and the nitty-gritty of getting you started on each of the individual social
media platforms.

The next few chapters enable you to hit the ground running on each of your preferred platforms. Even if you already have accounts set up and think you are ready
for Part III, "The 10-Step Method to Building a Fast and Effective Online Presence,"
we suggest you take a quick look through the following chapters as a refresher. You
might learn some new tricks, or perhaps we might influence you to launch your
brand on a new platform. Either way, the chapters provide a valuable reference that
you can dip into whenever you need help on a particular aspect of setting up and
managing your social media accounts. In fact, the details provided can make the
difference between an ordinary social media presence and something extraordinary.

Social Media
Networking Basics

3

Twitter: 140 Characters to Success

We came across the word "twitter" and it was just perfect. The definition was "a short burst of inconsequential information," and "chirps from birds." And that's exactly what the product was.

—Jack Dorsey, creator of Twitter

A Little History

Twitter started as a brainstorming session in 2006 when a group of board members at the podcasting company Odeo gathered with Mexican take-out in a children's park. The team involved included Jack Dorsey, who, over his burrito, came up with the idea of developing a *texting* or *Short Message Service* (SMS)-like system for communication between small groups of people. The idea seemed exciting—short bursts of content that fit in with the maximum number of characters permitted by SMS (most commonly 160). The team agreed on 140 characters to leave room for a username and a colon in front of the message. Although it was difficult at that time to explain the value, the team knew that they were on to something huge. Figure 3-1 shows the very first Twitter message, sent by Jack Dorsey (@jack).

(Source: Twitter.com)

Figure 3-1   The first ever Twitter message, sent by Jack Dorsey in March 2006.

What's been described as the *boom* moment for Twitter occurred during the *South by Southwest* (SXSW) festival in 2007. During the event, Twitter was showcased extensively via clever placement of two 60-inch plasma screens, which continually streamed Twitter messages (or *tweets* as they are now known). Suddenly, people got it! Hundreds of conference goers began keeping tabs on each other's whereabouts via the tweets being broadcast. It was the beginning of an exciting and addictive new world of communication and was quickly lauded by visitors, speakers, and every kind of blogger in attendance. The event culminated in the Twitter developers accepting the festival's award with the words, "We'd like to thank you in 140 characters or less. And we just did!"

Getting Started: Creating a Great Twitter Account

Getting started on Twitter is an incredibly simple process; making it great takes a little more gray matter. Here's how to do it right:

1. You can either go to Twitter.com and click the large yellow **Sign up** button on the lower right or go directly to twitter.com/signup, as shown in Figure 3-2. Click the **Sign up** button to get started.

2. Fill in the first field with your full name (see Figure 3-3).

(Source: Twitter.com)

Figure 3-2   The Twitter sign up screen.

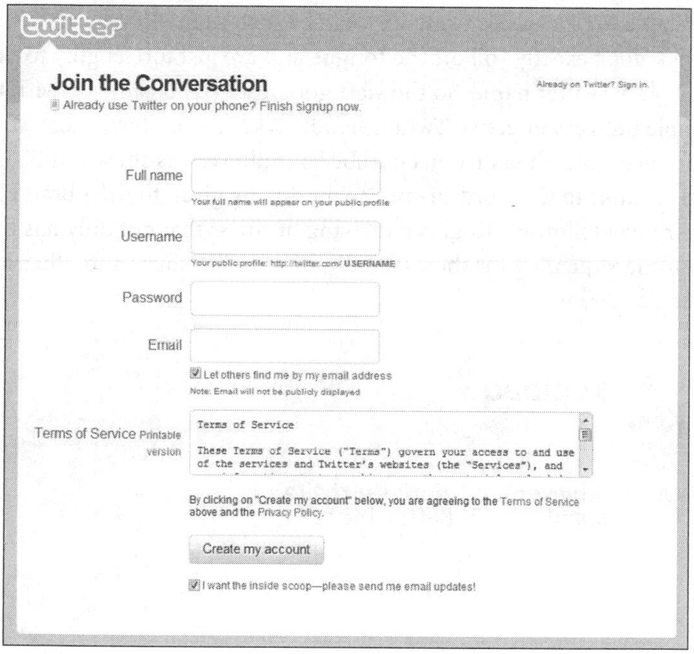

(Source: Twitter.com)

Figure 3-3   Twitter's Join the Conversation screen.

3. Select and enter your Twitter username (or handle). This is where you
    need to get creative and think of a name that truly sums up your brand
    and business.

You and your name may *be* the brand itself and ideal as your Twitter handle.

If you are an entrepreneur or a solo enterprise, you and your name may *be* the brand itself and ideal as your Twitter handle. Think about what your clients and customers will be looking for and then decide whether your chosen name will become easily recognizable to them. If you find your preferred name is already taken, start brainstorming and play around with key words and phrases that paint a verbal picture of your brand. And don't forget your company tagline; it might just contain the perfect Twitter name for you. It's also important to think about length of name because this can impact your tweets and the tweets of others dramatically by cutting back the number of characters available for messages. Company names such as the Korean BBQ Taco Truck don't exactly roll off the tongue and are just too lengthy to be used as a Twitter name. So the staff got creative and came up with the simple but very effective Twitter handle @kogibbq, which successfully translated into an enormous number of followers, as shown in Figure 3-4. Thanks to the word-of-mouse marketing given to their brand by their loyal followers, Kogi is a thriving business that not only has the customers queuing for their tacos, but for their t-shirts and other logo merchandise too.

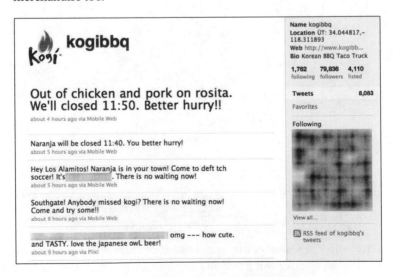

(*Source: Twitter.com*)

Figure 3-4 Korean BBQ Taco Truck adopted new names for their trucks and company t-shirts via their Twitter name.

4. Choose a strong yet memorable password. If multiple people regularly log in to the account, you may need to change the password often to ensure that ex-staff cannot gain access. Later in the book, we show you how *Cross Platform Promotion* (CPP) tools can be utilized to maintain control and security of your account, enabling you to have sole access to your password.

5. Enter your email address, making sure that you enter one that is in active use, because this will be used to verify and activate your account. At present, a single email address can be tied to only one Twitter account, so select with care.

6. Find sources that interest you. This is key to getting the most out of Twitter and will ensure that the information you seek about your brand arena is being tweeted directly to you. Select your areas of interest from the column on the left of the screen, and you'll see a number of suggested accounts for you to follow (see Figure 3-5). Simply click the **Follow** button along each suggested account that you want to follow, and you're on your way! A new list of suggested accounts will appear each time you select an interest. The green square above the list helps you to keep track of the number of accounts you are following. When you're done, just click the blue **Next: Friends** button on the lower-right of your screen.

> Finding sources that interest you is key to getting the most out of Twitter.

(Source: Twitter.com)

Figure 3-5 Finding sources that interest you is key to getting the most out of Twitter.

7. Find and follow your friends and contacts. Twitter can scan your email address book (if you wish) to find contacts who have Twitter accounts (see Figure 3-6). It's a quick and simple way to start building your network and is so easy to implement.

(Source: Twitter.com)

Figure 3-6   Twitter can search your email address books to find contacts you already know.

- Just type your email address and your email password into the boxes and then click **Find friends**. (Don't worry about giving this information away; Twitter doesn't store this login and won't use your email address without your permission.)

- A list of friends and colleagues who have Twitter accounts will appear, and then all you have to do is to follow them.

- You can follow all of them by clicking the blue **Follow All** button on the right side of the list or individually by using the gray **Send request** button next to their information.

- Click the **Next: others** button at the bottom of the screen, and a box will pop-up showing those contacts who aren't on Twitter and giving you the option to invite them by checking their individual boxes or by the clicking **Select all** button at the top of the screen.

8. To complete your sign up, use the Twitter search feature to search for anyone else you want to follow, like this:

- Type the name of the person you're searching for into the search box; a list of matching accounts will be shown, as illustrated in Figure 3-7. Click the **Follow** button next to those you want to begin following, and a confirmation message will appear.

- When you've finished following, just click the blue **Next set: you're done!** button to complete the process.

(Source: Twitter.com)

Figure 3-7   Use the Twitter search feature to find anyone else you would like to follow.

Voilà! You'll now be taken to your brand new profile page (also known as your timeline). This is where you can share information and begin tweeting.

Customizing Your Twitter Profile

Customizing your profile is a great way to make your brand stand out. As well as allowing you to include your company logo, Twitter lets you upload any image as your background, giving you the opportunity to present your business in a unique and personal way that expresses its brand personality.

Adding Your Logo or Photo to Your Profile

1. Start by clicking **Settings** in the upper-right navigation bar.

2. Now click **Profile**, which is the fifth tab along the top.

3. Click **Change Image**, along with the profile picture.

4. You'll see the **Choose File** button. Click this button to choose which file to load.

After you have selected your image file, click **Save** at the bottom of the page. Your thumbnail image will then appear, as shown in Figure 3-8.

The Profile tab also gives you the option to change your name, location, web details, and to enter a bio. Again, be creative here and let your brand personality shine. When you're happy with your profile, be sure to click the **Save** button at the bottom of the page.

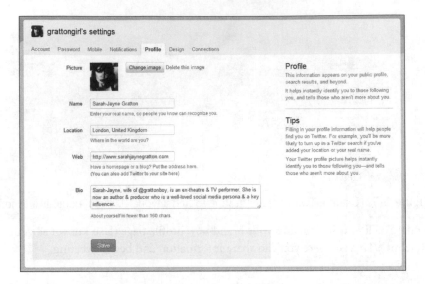

(Source: Twitter.com)

Figure 3-8   This is how @grattongirl's profile settings look.

Personalizing Your Background

There are many ways to personalize your profile by adding a creative background that effectively represents your business brand. Twitter provides a number of free designs that are a breeze to incorporate, as shown in Figure 3-9.

1. Log in to Twitter.com.

2. Click **Settings** under your username in your top navigation bar or go to twitter.com/account/settings.

3. Click the rightmost tab, labeled **Design**.

4. Select a template by clicking it or upload your own background image by clicking the **Change background image** button and selecting your preferred file; see @grattonboy's example in Figure 3-10.

    Again, this can be your logo, image of your products or offices, or whatever makes the best statement for you.

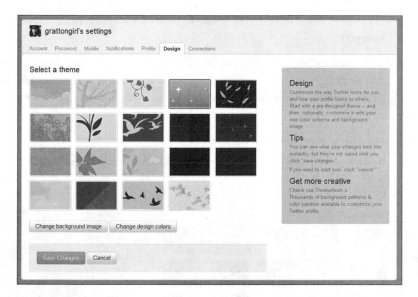

(Source: Twitter.com)

Figure 3-9   Twitter's background and color options are easy to incorporate into your profile.

(Source: Twitter.com)

Figure 3-10   @grattonboy chose to personalize his background with an image montage of his publications. You could easily do the same with your product range.

Always remember to save your changes when done (that is, click **Save Changes**).

If you want to customize the sidebar and font colors of your page, click **Change design colors**. You can play around with the various options until you are happy by clicking any of the boxes to change your colors (see Figure 3-11).

5. Click **Done** after making your choices.

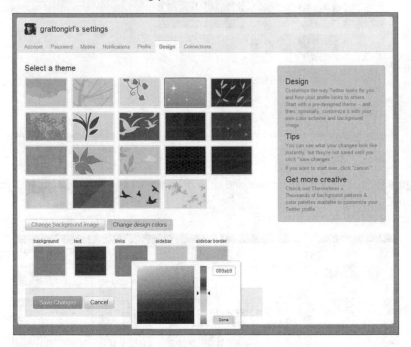

(Source: Twitter.com)

Figure 3-11   You can easily customize your colors using the tools provided by Twitter.

The previously mentioned options provided by Twitter are great for getting your feet wet, but if you want something with a little more oomph, you may want to flip forward to Chapter 15, "Step 6: Do You Need a Brand Makeover?" which recommends a number of other options that will help to make your Twitter profile truly unique.

So you're now ready to take your place in the Twitterverse. Part III of the book tells you everything you need to know about getting it right first time, from understanding the behavior of the Twitter arena to tweeting like a pro. If you can't wait to get started, you can skip to it right now. If however, you want to set up all your platforms before takeoff, then stay with us as we move on to the next big social media arena: Facebook.

4

Facebook Pages: The Public Face of Your Brand

More than 175 million people use Facebook. If it were a country, it would be the sixth most populated country in the world.

—Mark Zuckerberg, creator and CEO of Facebook

A Little History

Facebook was developed way back in early 2004 by Mark Zuckerberg, a sophomore at Harvard University. The name for Facebook, which he first introduced as the-facebook.com, came from the publication handed out to new students at the start of the academic year to help them get to know each other and make new friends: the Facebook.

At first it was exclusively a Harvard site, a way for Zuckerberg and the other students there to keep in touch via the Internet. This exclusivity didn't last long, however, as its popularity exploded in just a few months; and it was soon available to other colleges and high schools. The explosion continued to gain momentum, and a year later, Facebook, as it was by then known, was opened to all Internet users aged 13 and over.

Show Me the Money

Facebook has some weighty investors, including PayPal cofounder Peter Thiel, Accel Partners, and Greylock Partners. Microsoft, too, saw an opportunity and jumped onboard during 2007, investing $246 million for a 1.6% share. All the investors are looking to reap the rewards from the Facebook frenzy, but despite offers from Yahoo! and Google to buy Facebook, Mark Zuckerberg insists that it's not for sale!

A Constant Flow of New Features

Facebook has continued to evolve and improve the user experience, adding many new features to include a news feed, improved privacy options, notes, and importing tools, along with a plethora of available apps that grows on a daily basis.

Your Facebook Page is your brand window, working around the clock to showcase you and engage with customers and fans.

Why a Page and Not a Profile?

In Facebook's own words,
"Pages are for organizations, businesses, celebrities, and bands to broadcast great information in an official, public manner to people who choose to connect with them. Similar to profiles, Pages can be enhanced with applications that help the entity communicate and engage with their audiences and capture new audiences virally through

friend recommendations, News Feed stories, Facebook events, and beyond." (Source: Facebook.com)

In essence, Facebook is your brand window—a blend of an online fan club and publicity department, working around the clock to showcase and engage with your customers and fans. Having a Facebook Page makes it simple for both new and existing customers to find your business. It provides a superb marketing opportunity, allowing you to have as many fans as you are able to attract, and what's more, your Facebook Page will get picked up by search engines, creating even greater brand visibility.

Creating Your Facebook Page

Facebook offers a variety of Page options for every kind of business brand and individual, so take a look at these on the *Create a Page* section of their website (See Figure 4-1): www.facebook.com/pages/create.php.

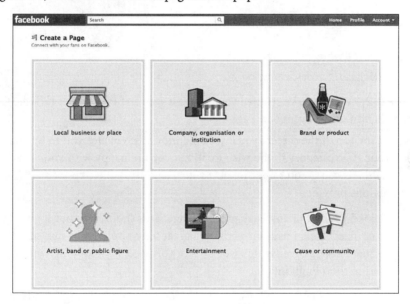

(Source: Facebook.com)

Figure 4-1   Facebook offers a wide variety of Page options.

Here are the essential steps to building your Page:

1. Select the type of Page that best suits your business or brand from the options provided (refer to Figure 4-1).

2. Fill out your Page name and select your type of business from the drop-down menus. When you're happy, click **Get Started**. You are then taken to your brand new Page, as shown in Figure 4-2.

(Source: Facebook.com)

Figure 4-2   When you've selected your business type and Page name, click the Get Started button to view your new Page.

3. At the top of the screen, you'll see an option that enables you to update your Page category if you wish to. When you are happy with your selection, you can go on to personalize your Page, using the step-by-step options provided.

4. Upload your company Page profile image. This should be your logo, a recognized press image, or perhaps a great team shot. If you can, select a square image because this won't distort or need any cropping when used in thumbnail images.

5. Invite your friends and fans. Here you can invite any existing friends on Facebook or important contacts from an address book to view your new Page in a similar way to Twitter's profile setup. We suggest leaving this step until after the Page is complete and up and running, but it's a good way of getting some initial numbers if you're feeling daring.

6. Next, click the Info tab (see Figure 4-3) to provide essential information about your company. Be sure to include your website address and contact information and provide a well-thought-out introduction or bio that lets others know all about your brand. Be sure to click the **Save Changes** button as you go along (see Figure 4-4).

(Source: Facebook.com)

Figure 4-3   Click the Info tab to the left of your new Page to enter your company information.

7. You can jazz up your Page through incorporating a number of apps that will add a variety of useful interactive features. To find the options available, click the **Apps** button on the left-side menu. A variety of options will now be presented to you, as shown in Figure 4-5. Feel free to experiment and try them all out; you can easily remove them later.

8. Now return to your main Page and click the **Photos** tab (see Figure 4-6) to upload photos of your products, team, or other images that best depict your business and brand. You may want to create several albums to reflect different aspects of your business or brand (as shown in Figure 4-7). If you are a service-related company, you might want to create albums with past events or team members' photos to create a feeling of warmth and approachability for new fans and potential customers.

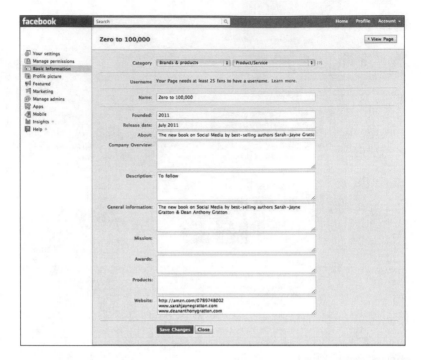

(Source: Facebook.com)

Figure 4-4   When you are happy with the basic information entered, be sure to save it by clicking the Save Changes button.

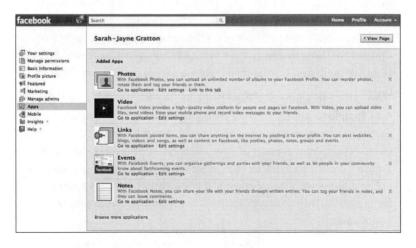

(Source: Facebook.com)

Figure 4-5   Selecting and adding Apps to your Facebook Page.

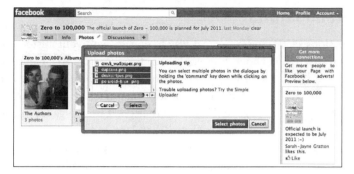

(Source: Facebook.com)

Figure 4-6   To add your photos, click the Select photos button.

(Source: Facebook.com)

Figure 4-7   Clicking the Photos button enables you to upload your images and categorize them into albums showing your products, services, events, or staff.

Using Discussions

The Discussions section offers a great way to engage with your customers. You can create a new discussion about different products or services (see Figure 4-8) and allow questions to be raised (and answered) on each particular aspect of manufacture, use, or user experience. This is another great way to gauge how you are doing in the marketplace and to gain support for forthcoming company events, special offers, or competitions. Discussions are like groups but a lot more public, and their content may even get picked up on the Internet. In Part III, "The 10-Step Method to Building a Fast and Effective Online Presence," we explain in more detail how to maximize your use of discussions.

> Discussions are a great way to gauge how you are doing in the marketplace.

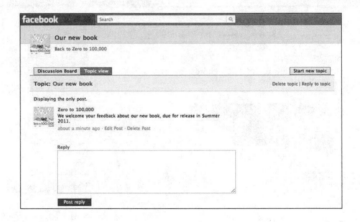

(Source: Facebook.com)

Figure 4-8   Using discussions is a great way to engage with your customers.

A number of great resources are available on Facebook itself to help you find your way around Pages. Just clicking the **Help** button and typing in "pages" will lead you to a huge list of questions and answers to guide you through the various options available to you via Facebook itself. There's also a great Page on Pages at www.facebook.com/FacebookPages that offers a wide range of resources and examples.

Enjoy finding your way around Facebook via your brand new business Page!

5

LinkedIn: Adding Your Link to the Chain of Success

LinkedIn as a Rolodex is the tip of the iceberg. It can do so much more, at so little cost, if only people knew!

—*emediawire.com*

A Little History

LinkedIn was founded in May 2003 by super-angel entrepreneur Reid Hoffman as a social networking site for professionals. Today, it has more than 90 million registered users in over 200 countries worldwide, with a new member joining every second and within excess of 47 million monthly visitors around the world.[1]

> LinkedIn is one of the only social media resources that's valuable without needing constant attention.

What's It All About?

The primary purpose of LinkedIn is to allow registered users to maintain a list of contact details of people they know and trust in business—if you like, a social media Rolodex. Many social media marketers overlook the importance of LinkedIn, but it's one of the only social media resources that is valuable without needing constant activity. Once your profile is created, it remains a strong professional presence, representing you quietly yet effectively with minimal input.

The people in your LinkedIn network are called *connections*, and after you sign up, you can invite anyone (whether a site user or not) to become a connection of yours.

These connections can then be used in a number of ways:

- To expand on previous connections through the introduction of connections to their connections (termed *second-degree connections*) and also the connections of second-degree connections (termed *third-degree connections*)

- To locate business opportunities recommended by connections in your network

- To list jobs and opportunities within your company or to seek new career opportunities through your connections

- To research companies, products, and services in a transparent way that allows sharing and engagement

- To share news about your business brand including photographs and links to external websites

1. Quantcast 2011.

LinkedIn Answers and Groups

LinkedIn Answers allows members to ask questions for the community to answer. The feature is completely free, and the identity of the people asking and answering questions is known.

LinkedIn Groups is a searchable feature that enables users to make new business relationships by joining alumni, industry, professional, or other relevant groups. LinkedIn groups can be created in any subject and by any member of LinkedIn. Alongside companies having their own profile pages, so too can specific groups of people with similar expertise and interests connect, share information, and collaborate on projects.

Getting Started on LinkedIn

Clearly, LinkedIn can be a powerful tool for your business. So like all those executives from the Fortune 500 companies who are members, start by completing the following steps to make sure that you have an impressive profile:

1. Login to LinkedIn.com, and you will be taken to the home page from where you can sign up (see Figure 5-1).

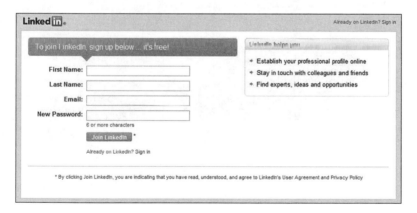

(Source: Linkedin.com)

Figure 5-1   The sign-up page from where you can join LinkedIn.

2. Sign up by completing the section Join LinkedIn Today. Be sure to give an active email address and a secure password.

3. When your details are added, click the **Join Now** button.

4. A page will open displaying the message, "Let's get your professional profile started." Here you'll need to provide details of your professional employment, country, industry, and so on. When you're happy with your entry, click the **Create my Profile** button to complete the initial process.

5. LinkedIn now offers to help you search for your existing contacts. By clicking **See Who You Already Know on LinkedIn**, you can check your existing contact address books in your email accounts (for example, Hotmail, Yahoo!, and Gmail). If you do not want to do this, you can opt to skip this step.

6. LinkedIn next confirms your email address by sending an email to the address you provided when you registered. Confirm this by clicking the link contained within it. So be sure to use a readily available email address when you first sign up.

7. After you've clicked the link, a new window opens, as shown in Figure 5-2. Click **Confirm**, and you'll be asked to sign in to LinkedIn with the email address and password you provided in step 2.

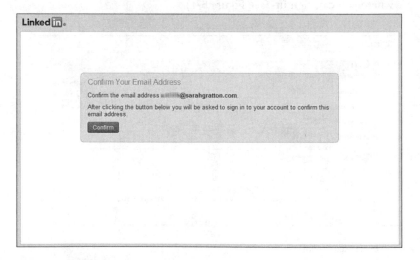

(Source: Linkedin.com)

Figure 5-2   You are taken to this window after you confirm your email address with LinkedIn.

Your new LinkedIn profile is now complete; see @grattongirl's profile page in Figure 5-3.

Congratulations! You're now a member of LinkedIn and can start connecting.

If you have impressed a colleague or business partner, you can invite that person to write a recommendation for you on LinkedIn that is visible to all your connections, as shown in Figure 5-4.

(Source: Linkedin.com)

Figure 5-3   @grattongirl's (a.k.a. Sarah-Jayne Gratton) completed LinkedIn page.

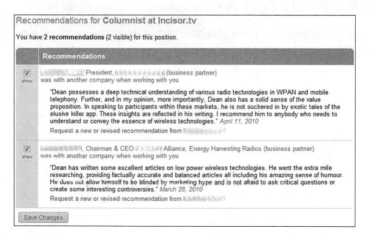

(Source: Linkedin.com)

Figure 5-4   LinkedIn recommendations, such as those shown for @grattonboy (a.k.a. Dean Anthony Gratton) can prove to be very effective for building trust between connections and potential business partners.

If anyone writes a reference that you're not happy with, you can choose not to display it on your LinkedIn profile.

A recommendation is a short paragraph detailing your exceptional qualities and what makes you a great person to work with; this is essentially a way of vouching for each other in the LinkedIn network. Incidentally, if anyone ever writes a reference that you are not happy with, you can just decide not to show it on your profile.

Not only can you impress people within the LinkedIn community, but having a profile on LinkedIn means you can also maintain control over what search results bring up about you. It can be useful to have a ready-made summary of information about you high up on the Google search results list, and you can find out more about this in Part III, "The 10 Step Method to Building a Fast and Effective Online Presence."

To Upgrade or Not to Upgrade

A possible disadvantage of LinkedIn is that not all of it is free. To see some people's profiles, you have to upgrade your membership. Similarly, when you search for people, you can look at only the first one hundred results if you're a free member. Upgrades start from around $25 per month; the more you upgrade your membership, the more results you can see and the more general access you get. Our advice is to start with the basic account; this is a sufficient platform for a great many businesses. If you do feel the need to upgrade, you can always do so later.

In Part III of the book, we show you how to maximize your LinkedIn presence and to make the most of every feature available.

6

YouTube: Your Brand Channel

We are in a YouTube society now.
—New York Times (2011)

A Little History

YouTube was founded by three former PayPal employees in 2005 and has never looked back! Based in San Bruno, California, it primarily showcases user-generated video content online, with registered users being able to upload an unlimited number of videos. YouTube was purchased by Google Inc. in 2006 for $1.6 billion, and the company now operates as a subsidiary of Google.

It's Big

Whereas many of us think of YouTube as a great hosting site for the next big viral video sensations, savvy entrepreneurs use the true benefit of YouTube to market their businesses and educate their customers.

After all, YouTube enables us to connect with an audience like never before and without the huge budgets needed to support our television-oriented efforts. Now we can freely share our expertise and knowledge using brains over budget to market and showcase our products and services.

So before we get started in establishing your channel, let's find out what YouTube really enables us to do:

- YouTube enables us to upload event presentations and slides in video format, to benefit those individuals who were not able to attend. This means that a local event can have a global audience.

- Both existing and potential customers or clients can be shown your company's expertise on its products and services and that knowledge is always just a click away from them. Many companies are now choosing to translate their user manuals and guides into instantly accessible video tutorials that provide a human touch to your brand.

- The relatively new Google Universal Search will also show YouTube video options when you search for a specific topic. Try using it to find videos on products and services like your own. You can utilize this great tool by ensuring that you use the right channel tags and keywords, which we discuss later in this section.

- YouTube videos offer you the opportunity to receive feedback comments and subscriptions—the ultimate tool and subsequent incentive for producing customer-friendly relations.

- Customer testimonials no longer need to be consigned to the filing cabinet or a static web page. By encouraging customers to send in their testimonials by video, you can create a community of enthusiasts who will become a 24-hour sales team, their endorsements being accessible to potential customers around the clock.

- Case studies can also be brought to life using YouTube, showcasing your professionalism and broadcasting your potential to millions every day.

By utilizing *Cross Platform Promotion* (CPP), which we unveil in Part III of the book, you can make your YouTube videos accessible across all the major social media platforms. In other words, "YouTube it, and they will come."

> YouTube testimonials allow you to create a community of enthusiasts who will become your 24-hour sales team.

Many people visit YouTube to carry out research into products and services and upload videos of their findings back on to YouTube. In the same way as the customer testimonials are posted (as mentioned earlier), so too can product reviews find their way to potential customers. Of course, this can be a double-edged sword, in that negative reviews are also freely available, which is why monitoring and responding to postings is vital to your maintenance of an effective and positive social media presence.

Getting Started

1. Decide on the username for your channel (your business name or perhaps a reflection of the products and services you offer). This should be a name that is, or will become, instantly recognizable with your brand.

2. Go to the YouTube Create Account page and enter your chosen username in the Username box, as shown in Figure 6-1.

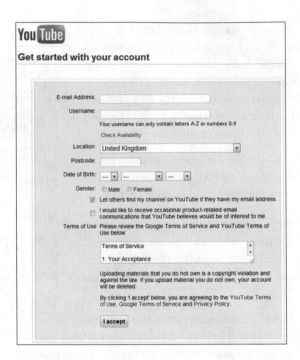

(Source: Youtube.com)

Figure 6-1   The YouTube Create Account page.

3. Either click the **Check Availability** link or move the cursor to another field.

4. Beside the username you entered, you will see either "Username unavailable" or "Username available." If your chosen username is unavailable, some alternatives will be suggested (see Figure 6-2). Alternatively, enter a new username choice, as in step 2.

5. When you've found a username you like, fill in the other boxes (or fields) to complete the signup process.

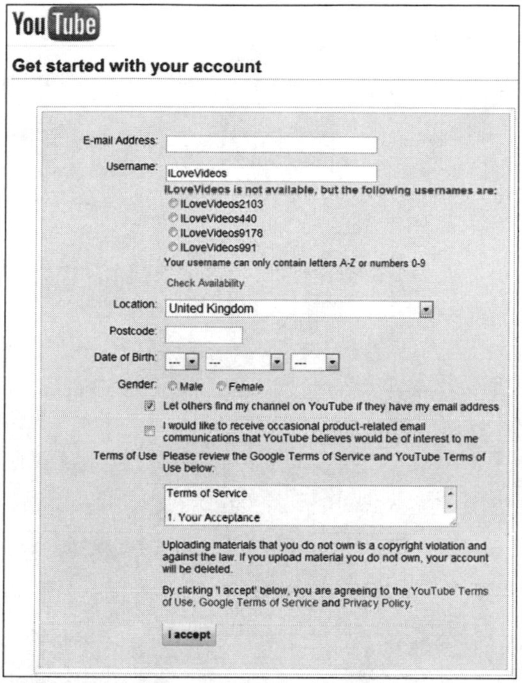

(Source: Youtube.com)

Figure 6-2   If your preferred username is unavailable, some available alternatives will be listed.

Customizing Your Channel

Now that you've registered with YouTube, you'll have the exciting task of customizing your channel. Branding or customizing your channel will make you look professional, and you'll gain more views and subscribers.

The first page you see when you view your channel will be quite gray and somewhat disconcerting (see Figure 6-3), but this will all soon change.

Start by clicking the **Settings** button. You'll be taken to an area where you can view your YouTube URL and channel name in all their glory. You'll now have the opportunity to add *channel tags*, which are basically key words from which users can find you. For example, if you are a coffee shop, the channel tags *coffee* and *shop* are obvious choices.

You can now select the type of account you want to present to the world. These are predominantly entertainment based, so as a business, you might want to stick with the YouTuber option.

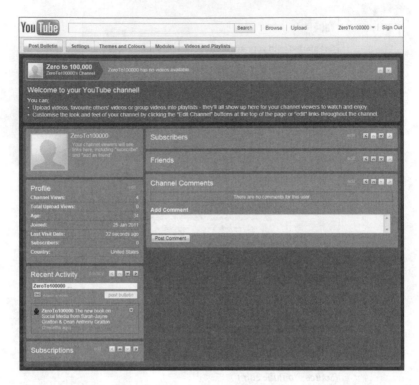

(Source: Youtube.com)

Figure 6-3 Your YouTube channel page will look something like this prior to customizing it.

You'll have the option to make the channel visible, but we suggest waiting until your channel is fully customized before doing so. The same principle goes for the option that you'll see just below the Channel Tags box, Let others find my channel on YouTube if they have my email address (see Figure 6-4).

(Source: Youtube.com)

Figure 6-4 Your YouTube channel's Settings options.

Don't forget to click the **Save Changes** button (in the lower-right corner of the window) to save and apply the updates you've just made.

Selecting a Channel Theme

1. Start by clicking the **Themes and Colors** tab, which will take you to a page of color theme options as shown in Figure 6-5. You can choose to select one of these themes for your channel or create your own individual theme.

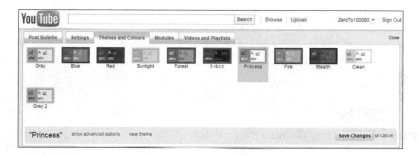

(Source: Youtube.com)

Figure 6-5   Themes and Colors section options.

2. When you click one of the color themes, the background of your channel changes to show you a preview of how your channel will look if you select it.

3. If you find a theme that you want to stick with and have displayed on your channel, click the **Save Changes** button to update your channel to that of your chosen theme.

4. If you don't like the theme you are seeing in preview, click **Cancel** or click another theme to change the channel background.

Making It Your Own

You can further customize your theme by clicking the **Show Advanced Options** button, which appears just below the standard color themes.

The window expands as shown in Figure 6-6 to display a variety of ways to create your own background theme. Customize by selecting different colors for the various aspects of your channel.

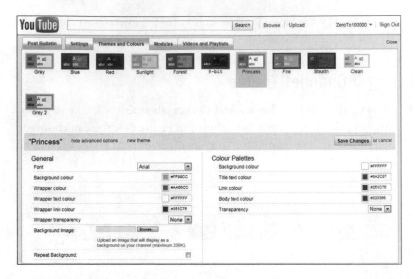

(*Source: Youtube.com*)

Figure 6-6 Selecting advanced theme options.

Adding a Background Image

1. Click the **Show Advanced Options** button, then click the **Browse** button beside the Background Image option (see Figure 6-6). Choose an image from your computer that works well as your channel's background. Select the image.

2. It will now appear centered on your channel page, and you can see a preview of how your channel will look with it included in this way. If you prefer to repeat the image across your channel's background, click and check the **Repeat Background** box (see Figure 6-7).

3. Click the **Save Changes** button to update your channel with these settings.

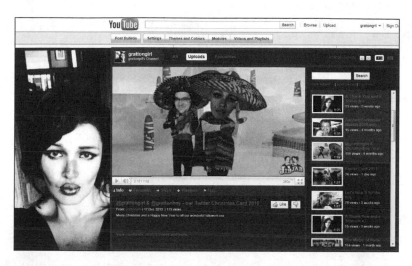

(Source: Youtube.com)

Figure 6-7   @grattongirl used a repeat background image to personalize her channel.

Managing Modules

To edit the modules/boxes that are displayed on your channel, you must click the **Modules** button, as shown in Figure 6-8. Various options will then be displayed.

(Source: Youtube.com)

Figure 6-8   Selecting which modules to display on your channel.

Choose the modules that you want to show on your channel, as shown in Table 6-1.

If you want to show one of these modules on your channel, click and select that option. Then click the **Save Changes** button to update your channel with the new modules now displayed.

Table 6-1   Channel Modules

The Different Modules You Can Display on Your Channel

Type	Description
Comments	Useful for customer feedback.
Friends	Here you can show team members or colleagues.
Subscribers	Useful to show who's following your channel.
Subscriptions	Shows who *you* subscribe to.
Recent Activity	Keeps track of what's happening on your channel.

If you *do not want to show one of these modules* on your channel page, click and uncheck the box next to that module option (so that the box is blank).

As always, be sure to click the **Save Changes** button to update your channel. You can change the location of your channel modules by locating the module you want to move and then clicking the arrow buttons in the right corner of the module to shift it either up, down, or across your channel page.

Your First YouTube Video

You may be surprised to learn that your first YouTube video is probably already made (or, at least on its way to being). If you have or work for a company that likes to make interesting slide shows and demonstrations of its products, or if you have footage of a recent product launch or even a number of great photos to make into a slide show, you're well on your way to launching the first video on your YouTube channel.

Your first YouTube video is probably already made.

The first thing you need to do is to make use of video-editing software. If you're a Mac user, you probably already have iMovie installed, which enables you to transform pretty much any existing footage, slide show, or images into a pretty decent video. If you're a Microsoft Windows user, take advantage of Microsoft's own video-editing options or invest in an easy-to-use editing package such as Cyberlink's Power Director, Sony Vegas Movie Studio, or Pinnacle Studio. You'll need these if you want to add an introduction in the form of an opening screen with titles, a voiceover (if needed), or maybe a little background music to set the scene, captions throughout (if necessary for clarification), and an ending screen with company details, to include your website and other contact information.

Think Simple

The best YouTube business videos are short, simple, and easy on the eye, so, don't try to be too clever with your production. Otherwise, you might end up with a piece that's too busy and confusing to get your brand message across.

Basic Rules for YouTube Success

These guidelines show you how to take a basic YouTube account and make it one of your strongest business tools.

- Remember that YouTube is a social platform, a community where two-way communication is standard practice. Your videos need to reflect your desire for feedback and the exchange of ideas and opinions.

- If you have a fresh and exciting team, capture their presentations and bring a sense of connection to your audience so that they almost feel a part of your team.

- Where possible, keep your videos under five minutes to maintain interest. Careful editing will keep the content fresh and relevant.

- Spread the word by taking advantage of YouTube's gigantic community and distribute your videos through emails and embeds. Encourage your subscribers on YouTube to spread the message at the end of each video you upload and on your channel page itself.

- Keep it real! Compelling and genuinely authentic videos frequently receive high view counts, while overly produced messages often fall flat.

- Stay in touch with what's going on and update supporters when you have a position on a breaking news story that relates to your business. This not only shows that you have your finger of the pulse of your particular arena, but it also marks you as an expert in the field.

- Get creative with question-and-answer videos that call for video replies from the YouTube community.

- Create incentives for viewers to upload videos about your products and services. Keep them engaged and motivated, and they will work to become your brand ambassadors.

Customizing Your Display of Videos and Playlists

After you've begun to upload your videos, you can choose to display and highlight the latest ones on your channel by clicking the **Video and Playlists** tab (see Figure 6-9). You can choose to display:

- All (playlists, uploads, and favorites)

- Just Uploads

- Just Playlists

- Just Favorites

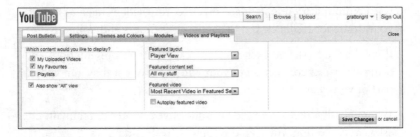

(Source: Youtube.com)

Figure 6-9   Customizing which videos and playlists are displayed.

In Part III of the book, "The 10 Step Method to Building a Fast and Effective Online Presence," you'll find additional tips and tricks to help you get the very best out of YouTube.

7

Foursquare: Putting Your Brand on the Map

Foursquare is focused on growth...getting merchants to think about the Internet is a big step.

—Dennis Crowley, founder of Foursquare

A Little History

Foursquare (Foursquare.com) has taken the social media world by storm over the past year. The service was created in 2009 by former mobile gaming designer Dennis Crowley and Naveen Selvadurai. As of December 2010, the company reported it had five million registered users.[1]

What Makes Foursquare Different?

Foursquare is different from the other platforms in that it offers a new blend of geo-tagged social networking, status updates, business review, and location-based gaming. If you're not already familiar with it, take the time to get to know it now, as it may turn out to be a great business ally.

Unlike the other social media platforms covered in this book, Foursquare is first and foremost an *app* that runs on your location-aware mobile device. It enables users to find out what's around them in the "real world," share their activities and locations with their contacts, and compete with each other by earning points and unlocking badges. Foursquare's ever-increasing popularity provides a great opportunity for businesses to promote themselves to a new audience and a new way to reward loyal customers.

It's worth mentioning here before you read on that Foursquare isn't a great platform for all businesses. As you will glean from the following, at present, it is predominantly used by bars, restaurants, and coffee shops, so depending on your business, it might not be the right platform for you.

Getting Started with Foursquare

Foursquare offers two types of platform for businesses. The first is the venue/merchant platform, from where special offers and incentives can be made directly via the venues themselves. The second is brand promotion using badges (as shown in Figure 7-1).

---

1. Merino, Faith, "Dennis Crowley: Foursquare now has 5M users," VatorNews, August 2010.

(Source: Foursquare.com/business)

Figure 7-1   The two types of business options provided by Foursquare.

To get started, log on to foursquare.com/business, and the two options will appear. Now just select the best option for you, and Foursquare will provide a mini-tutorial, showing exactly what each of the business services offers and allowing you to sign up there and then. If you are a merchant or venue, you can immediately search for your virtual place on Foursquare using their **Search and claim your venue** button (see Figure 7-2).

In addition to driving business through specials and brand badges, signing up for Foursquare's free merchant platform also allows you access to your Venue Stats dashboard, enabling you to track your customer foot traffic over time (see Figure 7-3).

Foursquare's merchant platform enables you to track your customer traffic over time and is a great social metric tool.

(Source: Foursquare.com/business/venues)

Figure 7-2 Foursquare's merchant platform allows you to search and claim your venue in the virtual world.

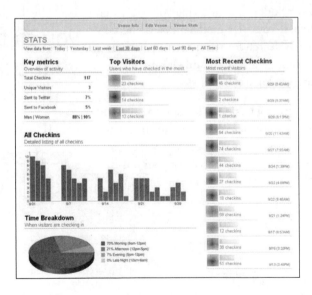

(Source: Foursquare.com)

Figure 7-3 Foursquare enables merchants to view their stats, which include top visitors and most recent checkins.

How to Get the Best Out of Foursquare

1. **Provide near-to checkin offers:** When Foursquare users enter a business, one of the first things they do is *checkin* via the Foursquare app on their mobile device. This alerts the user's friends, telling them where the user is and offering them points. When users do this, they're also telling Foursquare their exact location. Because of this, Foursquare offers a service that allows businesses that are nearby to promote themselves. For example, if you run a coffee shop close by, you can set up a system via Foursquare that sends a message to anyone who checks in to your business. This message can (and should) include some kind of promotion via notification on Foursquare, such as "We see that you just checked in to Ray's Bookstore down the street. When you're done, stop by the Happy Coffee Shop for a free slice of cake with any two coffees ordered."

2. **Give rewards for new checkin customers:** Another neat trick of Foursquare is its ability to track how many times a user has checked in to a place. So to encourage new business, why not do a promotion that rewards users for their first checkin at your business?

3. **Discounts for recommendation:** Foursquare users are heavily encouraged to leave recommendations (or tips), as shown in Figure 7-4. They are garnered by businesses offering incentives, such as "10% off your bill if you show the cashier that you have just posted a favorable tip." Businesses participating in Foursquare are also given the ability to post sponsor tips about their own venues or what to do in the area.

4. **Reward the Mayor of your Foursquare venue:** Foursquare effectively keeps track of who's checked in to your business the most, and that person is deemed to be the *Mayor*. This can create real excitement and competition among users while at the same time keeping customers coming back to earn their Mayorship. It can work wonderfully well for those businesses that encourage and promote this activity. We've seen several restaurants and bars achieve this by offering to buy the Mayor's first beer on each visit for as long as he remains Mayor. Figure 7-5 shows an example of this.

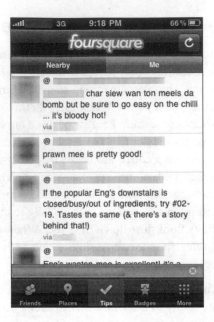

(Source: Foursquare.com)

Figure 7-4   Foursquare encourages merchants to reward users who give recommendations or tips.

(Source: Foursquare.com)

Figure 7-5   You can reward the Mayor of your venue with exclusive offers.

5. **Sponsored badge:** Another great way to promote your business is by
    sponsoring a badge (see Figure 7-6). Foursquare users earn badges
    based on their platform activity. There are many badges built in to the
    system already, but businesses are free to sponsor their own. As an
    example, let's say you own a chain of bakeries in your community. You
    could sponsor a badge that users can only earn after they've checked in
    to each individual store.

(Source: Foursquare.com)

Figure 7-6   Badges are a great way to spread your brand identity.

Foursquare has definitely brought home the business benefits of location-based
social networking, and with companies such as Facebook and Yelp both trying to
create their own versions based on its success to date, it's pretty obvious this type of
platform is here to stay.

So now that you have all you need to make a decision about choosing the best platforms for your brand and the knowledge to get started on each of them, it's time to
move on to another hugely important social media marketing tool: your blog.

8

Blogging Your Way to Business Success

This is the age of the blog! An age when even the President of the United States has seized the importance of this global phenomenon, appealing to those new-age bloggers among us to support his campaign values.[1] *But, blogging is actually nothing new. Ever since the first cavemen drew on walls, the need to document and share our thoughts and experiences in an attempt to make meaning of them has been a strong force within us.*

---

1. Source: http://dailycaller.com/2010/10/28/president-obamas-liberal-blogger-chat/

> Studies suggest that blogs are depended on more today for factual review than their traditional news counterparts.

Now, billions of journal entries later, we find ourselves using keyboards rather than quills and writing content using technology-integrated new media that has revolutionized the way we source and exchange information.

In Blogging We Trust

With this firmly in mind, we're about to shed some light on what many in the traditional media regard as a bone of contention, primarily out of fear of losing their advertising revenue (and let's face it, who can blame them?). There's no doubt that today's blogs pack an enormous amount of clout among their subscribers, and some studies suggest that blogs such as Mashable (Mashable. com) and The Huffington Post (Huffingtonpost.com) are becoming more trusted for factual review than their traditional news counterparts. Certainly, social media routes have taken precedence in terms of immediacy in reporting events; but now, more than ever, they have also become trusted allies in a crowded media-centric world.

So why exactly has this shift occurred so profoundly? Well, one train of thought points to the *likeness* factor (that is, the tendency for people to assume that random people on the Internet are like themselves). It makes sense as, when you strip away the physical vestiges of race, class, gender, and style, people seem more than willing to assume that others they meet online are fairly similar to themselves, and this in itself builds an immediate sense of trust and empathy. With this thought in mind, it seems that where advertisers have been going wrong all these years is in trying to "buy" the public's trust, which never quite works and is only ever one wrong move away from disgrace. And you don't always need to earn it either. It seems the big secret to gaining trust is to get people to believe that you share their perspective and understand their experiences.

It's not all cause for celebration, however, certainly in terms of business blogging, where, for the most part, we're still getting it wrong. The research group Forrester[2] found that of all blog content, people are inclined to believe corporate blogs the least; and when we consider the evidence, there's an obvious reason for this. Corporate blogs are often written by a sales team in disguise, and like those traditional advertisers before them, they are using their blogs as a means to continually pitch their products to the public, a method of marketing that we know just doesn't work anymore.

> Don't make the mistake of turning your blog posts into blatant sales pitches. This method of marketing will deter readers from subscribing to your blog.

So how do you put together a business blog that will not only be taken seriously but be trusted and shared by its readers and even picked up on the wider net to bring in new subscribers? This chapter shows you how to construct and manage the perfect blog for your brand that attracts rather than repels and creates a buzz that brings about a greater awareness of your business and its related products and services.

Using Your Head and Your Resources

Choosing the right platform and foundations for your blog begins with some fundamental decisions based on both your blogging requirements and the resources that you may already have within your business. Several key checkpoints need to be considered when formulating a successful blogging mission statement:

---

2. "Time to Rethink Your Corporate Blogging Ideas," by Josh Bernoff (Forrester Research)

- Determine posting frequency.

- Define how the blog should support the business.

- Understand your audience.

- Assign writers/researchers to be brand ambassadors.

- Set and follow word-count limits.

Each of these checkpoints is expanded on here.

How Often Should You Post?

First and foremost, you need to decide just how often you intend to post a new blog. "How on earth do I do that?" you ask. "What's the magic formula for success?" we hear you cry. Well, there's no definitive answer, and again, there's no one-size fits all philosophy, so let's start with some key issues.

What Do You Want to Gain from Your Blog?

Increasing your blog readership is a goal in itself, of course; but how should your blog work to support your overall business goals, and will it be a fundamental part of your marketing strategy? For example, if your website itself is a business genera-tor, a good blog will provide it with additional credibility and references gained from reviews and accompanying stories and comments. The majority of people read a blog because they want to expand their knowledge about a particular subject or area of their lives in a way that will add value. Knowledge is a powerful personal currency and one that most of us have a need to build through expanding our understanding of those things that have a positive effect upon us. What we as busi-nesses and brands ultimately need to gain from our blogging endeavors is our own post power stream; one that provides added value for our readers and positions us as authorities within our particular sectors. Our editorial foundations for this will be found through careful analysis of what our audience requires, in particular those aspects of our business or brand that might be questioned or misunderstood. Wherever possible, we need to provide answers to the most common questions in a way that delivers fresh, engaging, and valuable insights to create a continual buzz and generate an active following.

Who Is Your Audience?

By now, you should already know the answer to this question. The process behind setting up your other key social media platforms should have firmly cemented it into your psyche. Now it's time to re(de)fine your audience in terms of blog appeal. How much time do you suppose most of them will have to read blogs, and how active are they themselves in the blogging arena? What times of the day are they most likely to sit and read your blog? Remember that building a successful blog is like establishing a new community based on common interests and values. Instilling this sense of community among your subscribers will help to ensure its popularity and long-term appeal. Chapter 14, "Step 5: Instilling a Sense of Community," expands on this key point and helps you gain a further understanding about what can be achieved simply through the effective use of social media.

Who Are Your Brand Ambassadors?

Group blogs dramatically reduce the likelihood of burnout and are a great way for various members of your staff to become brand ambassadors, injecting their personalities into the posts and making them sparkle with team spirit. Identify those persons in your business who have a gift for communication and give their writing the chance to shine through your blog. Their individual personalities should be tailored to specific areas of the blog, based upon areas of expertise, so that they blend into one harmonious blogging symphony that will both inform and generate a response from your subscribers. Think of sectioning of your blog in the same way that you would segment a newspaper or magazine and allocate specific topics to the same brand ambassadors' post after post to maintain consistency in writing style and blog personality.

Limit your blog posts to 500 words or less to attract and maintain reader interest.

Size Isn't Everything, Is It?

Think about the most memorable blogs you've read. Revisit them and note their word counts. You'll probably notice a common thread: Less is definitely more in the realm of the successful blog. With this in mind, remember to keep your blog posts concise and relevant without rambling or straying from your core message. It's tough to engage busy people, and interest can be quickly lost when your word count goes beyond 500. This means that a certain amount of post tailoring is always required, but it's a skill quickly mastered and full of rewards in terms of subscribers and reposts.

Moving Forward

Now that you have your blogging team in place, you can move forward and begin planning your initial and subsequent blogs.

Design and Platform

Looks are important! A clean and professional look for your blog will entice a potential subscriber to read on. If your budget allows, by all means employ the services of a professional designer to ensure that your blog has the best possible layout and design. If you already use a web designer, talk to him or her about tying in the look and feel of your blog to your site design.

If your budget won't stretch to using a professional company to design your blog, the next best option is to use one of the low-cost or free theme templates that are available from popular blogging platforms such as WordPress (Wordpress.com), Tumblr (Tumblr.com), Blogger (Blogger.com), Posterous (Posterous.com), and TypePad (Typepad.com), as shown in Figure 8-1.

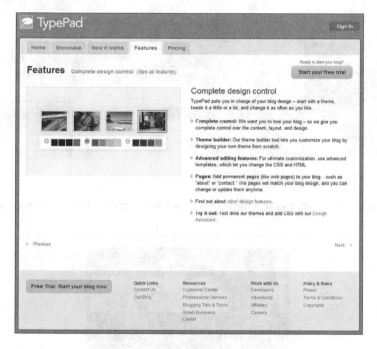

(Source: Typepad.com)

Figure 8-1   TypePad takes you step-by-step through the process of selecting and customizing a template, making it easy for first-time bloggers.

All of these platforms are designed to make life easier for bloggers and take you step-by-step through the process of launching your blog. Each platform has its own quirks and advantages, so the best advice is to check them all out and make a decision that best suits your business needs.

After signing up to your chosen platform, you'll have a gallery of ready-made templates to select a design from (see Figure 8-2). Pick a color scheme and layout that ties in (wherever possible) with your logo and company message. Compare the different options available and see how well they tie-in with your business personality as @grattongirl did. Her blog reflects her unique personal brand, as shown in Figure 8-3. The predefined layouts can all be easily personalized, and all the platforms mentioned in this chapter provide step-by-step guides to painlessly customize your blog.

(Source: Onebuckebook.com)

Figure 8-2   Try out a variety of themes to see which style fits best with your business message.

(Source: grattongirl.wordpress.com)

Figure 8-3   The @grattongirl blog ties in the profile message of Sarah-Jayne so that her followers and readers will instantly recognize her.

Content Planning

Work with your blog team to create an editorial calendar for your blog posts. Use it as a guide to ensure that your blogs are written on time and are fresh and relevant to your forthcoming products and promotions, but keep it flexible, as industry news and product/service revisions can change as time goes by. For example, blog posts surrounding the launch of a new product or service could be scheduled before, during, and after the event to cover the build-up, launch itself, and feedback following its release.

The Editorial Process

The editorial process can either be an elaborate or very simple affair, according to the size and scope of your business. A small business owner, for example, might follow this checklist to successfully plan content for his or her blog:

1. Brainstorm a list of content to publish.

2. Define dates and times when posts will be published.

3. Write each post in accordance with the publication schedule.

4. Edit and publish each piece.

A larger, corporate web team might have a more complex and flexible blog publishing process, like this:

1. Brainstorm a list of content to publish. Specify where and when the content should be published for a set time period. Include backup content items for each item set for publication and specify breakpoints to determine whether to delay or kill any content item.

2. Assign each piece of content based on the editorial calendar. Applications such as Google Calendar (see Figure 8.4) make it easy for group editing and approvals.

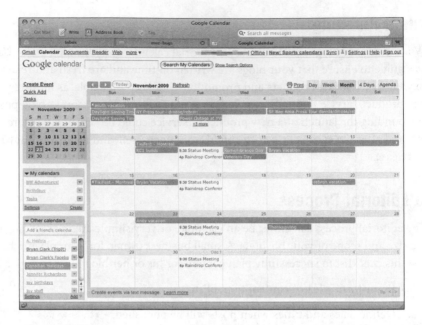

(Source: Google.com)

Figure 8-4   Google Calendar offers an effective way to produce an editorial calendar for your blog that can easily be shared and amended.

3. Produce each piece of content in accordance with the blog team assignment.

4. Review the first draft of each piece of content.

5. Give approval based on first draft edits (and adjust publication schedule if needed).

6. If approved, finish writing each piece of content and submit the draft.

7. Perform the final edit, copy edit, fact checking, and rewrites as needed.

8. Submit for review by legal team.

9. Make changes if/as needed based on legal input.

10. Submit content formally to your layout team (or blogging service).

11. Review content on the development server (published by blogging service or in-house team) and make changes if needed.

12. Publish the content on the production server.

Whatever the size of your company, a well-constructed production process will help you get the most out of your blog.

The Blog Post Process

After you've agreed on the best production process for your business size, it's time to plan how each individual blog post will be created. You should also have a process in place to time manage and control each post. For example, an interview with a partnering company for a particular piece will require a number of initial emails in preparation, as well as time to refine any questions, interview your subjects, obtain clarifications, and write up the interview. This all needs to be allowed for in your editorial calendar.

Make time to document the different processes for each type of content you publish. For example, determine how much research is needed prior to writing, whether interviews are involved (which might incur time delays), and whether permissions are needed for photographs, logos, charts, and so on. Some types of blog post preparation have an identical process, but don't assume they do. Sit down and map out the content-creation process to be 100% certain. This step alone will help avoid delays in your publishing schedule.

Sourcing and Building Great and Original Content

It's important to keep your content fresh and relevant to your subscribers' interests. The problem with many business blogs, however, is that they can easily become dry, stale, and repetitive. With this in mind, we've put together some simple exercises to help you and your blog team think creatively outside of the corporate box and make your posts really stand out and get noticed:

- Write a profile post on someone fundamental to your business.

- Select a popular blog post within your business arena (products/services) that you agree with and expand on the idea within it, linking to the original article and inviting comments.

- Find a popular blog post within your business arena that you disagree with and proactively deconstruct the idea, remembering again to link to the original.

- Find an iTunes podcast that relates to your business arena and write a review. Be sure to also post a link to your blog and brief summary of your review on iTunes as a way of thanking the creators of the podcast for their content.

- Ask a question relating to your business arena on Yahoo! Answers and document the responses in a blog post.

- Think of a how-to question related to your business and see whether it is answered in a YouTube video. Write about the question and embed the YouTube video within the blog. (We talk more about embedding videos later on in Chapter 9, "The Secrets to a Successful Blog.")

- Write a blog composed of positive customer reviews of your services/products. Consider using scans of thank you letters, photos from users, and responses from company questionnaires as fillers.

- Create a company horoscope blog, using the start date of your company as its birthday. Read your company horoscope and use it as the basis of a blog to talk about your services, team, and any forthcoming events in a fresh and entertaining way.

9

The Secrets to a Successful Blog

The most memorable blogs, business or otherwise, are written with soul and authenticity—in other words, those that are personal. You and your chosen blog team should all be passionate about your business, and this passion needs to consistently come across in your company blog posts.

Be a Font of Knowledge

Whatever the focus of your post, try to be as useful as humanly possible. By this, we mean that you should endeavor to create a resource for your particular field like no other out there. This doesn't mean producing posts full of staid facts and figures, but ones that intelligently and concisely inform while keeping your readers entertained. Use your blog as an opportunity to create a resource that's unique to your arena, to explore new angles, to provide tips and tricks, and to reward your subscribers with an ongoing stream of valuable information.

Remember It's a Two-way Street

A good blog should be a conversation, starting with your post of course, but continuing on with comments from readers and other bloggers. Get the conversation stirred up by posting questions, polls, and contests for your subscribers. Getting others involved in your blog is the best possible way to ensure it is passed along, mentioned in other social networking platforms, and listed higher in search engine rankings. This involvement also provides material for future posts and perhaps additional blogs based on responses, comments, and so on. These subsequent blogs will become self-generating promotions for your blog and ultimately your business.

Keep Consumer Problems in Mind

As already mentioned in Chapter 8, "Blogging Your Way to Business Success," it's important to consider what your customers are looking for in your business arena and to target a philosophy of posts geared toward attracting them. What problems do they have that need to be solved? Your solutions to these problems should form the basis of many of your blog posts, and you should be as useful as possible in answering them. To get a start on this, read other blogs with the same target audience and see what questions the readers are asking. You'll undoubtedly find a wealth of potential blog post titles from these alone.

Keep Them Wanting More

Ask yourself why you would come back to a blog and what qualities would lead you to subscribe to one. With a wealth of choices available in terms of content, what will make your blog stand out and entice a reader to return? The answer is simple: You need to give your readers a *reason* to return based on amazing content that you put out from day one and continue to consistently produce on a regular basis. Build a sense of anticipation wherever possible, linking one blog to another and whetting your subscribers' appetite for more in future posts. Keep them wanting more, and they'll keep coming back for more.

Make Headlines

You might create the most amazing blog post ever written, but if you accompany it with a poorly thought-out headline or title, your subscribers probably won't read on. As far as readers are concerned, headlines are the equivalent to movie trailers for your blog. Remember that your posts will be found around the Web and that it's the headline that draws an audience in initially, so always put some thought into the first words that potential readers and subscribers will see to ensure that you capture their interest and keep it. Pay attention to the popular headlines on other blogs and deconstruct them to analyze what works and why.

A Picture Paints a Thousand Words

Each of the popular blogging platforms makes it easy to add images into your posts. Wherever possible, use pictures that strengthen your message, create and maintain interest, and translate easily across the Web when reposted. When using any external image, check the copyright to be sure that the content owner allows it to be used.

Reinvention Is the Key to Longevity

Another key to long-term social media success lies in keeping your content fresh and relevant. That means not being afraid to diversify it and its style of delivery from time to time. Your blog will undoubtedly become stale if you do the same thing over and over again. When you sense that this is happening, be sure to re-evaluate your content and break out of the cycle. Explore other mediums such as movies and magazines for new ideas and keep your eyes and ears open for blogging inspiration. We look more at this important aspect of social media longevity in Part III of the book, "The 10-Step Method to Building a Fast and Effective Online Presence."

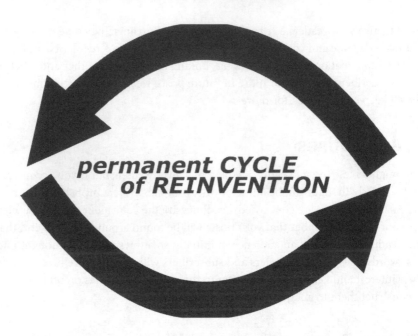

How to Presell Your Blog Content

With so many blogs out there for the picking, it's vital that you promote your blog as effectively as possible to as many potential readers and subscribers as possible. You can start doing this even *before* your blog goes live by proving your authority/knowledge in your particular business arena. Always remember that when promoting your site it's important to presell your content. Blogs are all about proving you can provide value to a reader in a particular niche. If you achieve this, it's easy to turn a casual browser into a loyal subscriber.

So let's get started with these great ways to presell your blog.

Strategize Your Blog Comments

As already mentioned, leaving comments on other popular industry blogs is a great way to acknowledge your expertise in a particular arena. Unfortunately, many businesses do this without a strategy. The trick is to ask questions that require a response and add real value to the post being discussed. Leaving a simple "thank you" remark won't attract much interest or traffic to your own blog. Make your comments stand out and be noticed by both the blog creator and other visitors to that blog. Always think in terms of initiating a response and bringing something fresh to the post that hasn't already been covered. When your own blog is underway, consider using a *plugin* (discussed later in this chapter) to automatically add a link to a complementary post on your blog site. Plugins draw people in and work like a shuttle to instantly transport new readers to your site.

Feature and Contribute Guest Posts

Your blog needs to attract an audience of subscribers who will, over time, translate into customers and advocates of your brand. So, invite prominent guest bloggers from your industry sector and promote their posts *prior* to publication to bring in a wealth of readers who already follow their posts and who are now an eager audience for your blog.

Similarly, become a guest poster on other well-known industry blogs to establish your credibility and attract readers to your own blog site. When it comes to guest posting, don't make the mistake of sending rehashed posts from your own blog. Your contributions need to be fresh and provide genuine benefit to the reader that leaves them feeling that they have gained something valuable from reading your contribution. If you achieve this, they will be keen to visit your own blog to learn more from your expertise.

Tweet Your Posts

Use your Twitter account to acquire a list of followers who will be interested in reading your blogs. Again, the trick here is to stand out from the crowd by interacting, retweeting, and asking questions. You want to continually tweet posts that are useful and establish your credibility in your market sector. After you've built your reputation, you can start to provide links to your blog posts that you feel your followers might find helpful. Tying in your blog posts to your tweets is fundamental to successful *Cross Platform Promotion* (CPP), which we cover in greater detail in Chapter 17, "Step 8: Introducing Cross Platform Promotion."

Use Your Facebook Page

Facebook can be an incredible way to market your blog. Again, interaction is the key here. You want to post questions on your page and describe what's going on in your new blog in a way that draws interest without coming across as a hard sell or pushiness. Offer links to your best posts that tie in to questions asked and answered on your page. Incorporate responses from those who post on your Facebook page into blog posts wherever possible to draw the reader in. The secret is to make readers feel that you are writing the piece specifically for them.

Create a sense of community within your Facebook page and make it a warm and convivial place to visit. Find out more about aspects of your industry and relay them to your readers in a way that continues to add value to your blog.

Use Personalized Recommendation Engines

Wikipedia (wikipedia.org) describes the likes of StumbleUpon (Stumbleupon.com) and Digg (Digg.com) as "Internet communities that allow users to discover and rate Web pages, photos, and videos. They are personalized recommendation engines which use peer and social-networking principles."

Correct use of these communities can prove to be an immensely powerful method to bring new readers to your blog (see Figure 9-1 and Figure 9-2).

(Source: Stumbleupon.com)

Figure 9-1   StumbleUpon is an Internet community and personalized recommendation engine that can bring significant traffic to your blog.

(Source: Digg.com)

Figure 9-2   Digg is another personalized recommendation engine that can bring a significant number of potential subscribers to your blog.

You gain respect through these communities by interacting with other users. In this particular instance, it's important to recommend other people's posts and create a network of users who will vote on your posts. The posts with the best titles are the ones that get clicked the most so, as mentioned previously in this chapter, you definitely want to write headlines that create curiosity and get you noticed.

Value-Added Blogging Tools

A variety of tools enable bloggers to add value and additional creativity to posts. We provide an overview of the most popular and useful tools available, but first let's start by clarifying a topic of confusion for many.

The confusion surrounds the difference between a plugin and a widget. Basically, plugins aren't meant to function on their own, being extensions to existing blogging applications. Their purpose is to enhance the functionality of your blog by offering functions and features that can be customized to suit your blog's individual purpose. Widgets are like plugins in that they allow you to easily add design elements to your blog by dragging and dropping the ones you want to include. Think of widgets as blog jewelry, visible to your audience and providing creative and fun features to your posts.

Plugins

As previously mentioned, plugins extend the base functionality of your blogging platform and can be used to track statistics, generate random quotes, and more. Each platform has its own plugin directory (see Figure 9-3) where you can view the various options. Experiment with them to find out more about what they can offer in terms of value for your blog.

Be aware that different themes support different plugins and that not all of them will work with your chosen look and feel.

(Source: Wordpress.com)

Figure 9-3   WordPress offers an extensive Plugin Directory with a multitude of options to enrich your blog.

Widgets

Widgets are used to add fun and interesting functional and visual elements to your blog. They appear in your blog's sidebar and display information that can be pulled from your blog or from other sources such as Facebook and Twitter.

WordPress offers a very simple and easy to use Widgets directory (see Figure 9-4) that lists each widget alphabetically in its own blue bar. An Interactive Widgets box at the bottom allows you to store widgets you have customized without losing their information, which is a very useful time-saving tool.

To select a widget, all you need do is to choose the one you prefer and drag it across into the sidebar. As you drag it, a box appears in the sidebar to drop in your chosen widget. Once there, it can be opened for you to customise if necessary, or you can simply save it.

You can move your widgets around into different positions in your sidebar by dragging them to your desired location. The other widgets will move out of the way and create a space for the moving widget.

(Source: Wordpress.com)

Figure 9-4   WordPress provides a Widgets section on their dashboard that gives an explanation of each widget they offer.

Really Simple Syndication

Really Simple Syndication (RSS) allows interested readers to follow your blog through their search engine readers or via an email subscription service that sends your latest blog posts directly to their Inboxes. In addition, every time you create a post, a link to it is posted on Facebook, Twitter, or another relevant social networking location you have selected or activated. Your followers or readers can then see your latest blog post as soon as it is created, instead of having to search the Internet to find it. It's like broadcasting to the virtual world that you have a new post available and automatically sending out a notice to whoever is interested in reading it.

We have favored Google's RSS process and tools here because many consider it to be the de facto standard, and it is an extremely easy system to adopt. First of all, you need to set up a Google (Google.com) account if you don't have one already (see Figure 9-5). Then go to FeedBurner (Feedburner.google.com) and sign in with your Google account.

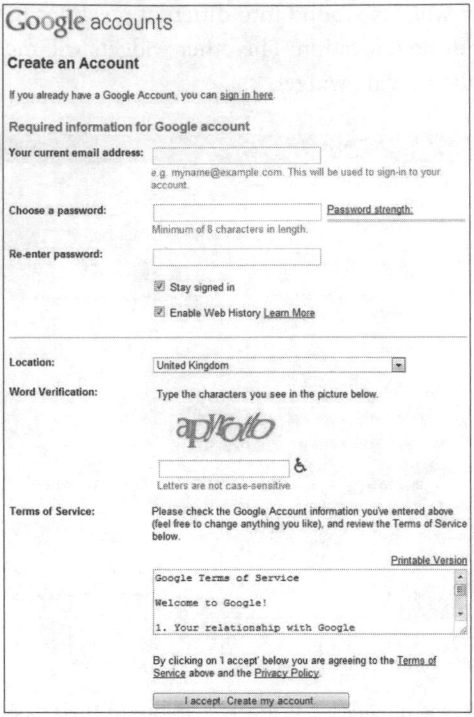

(Source: Google.com)

Figure 9-5   Start your RSS process by creating or signing into a Google account.

After you are logged in, you will see the My Feeds page, as shown in Figure 9-6. Type in your blog's URL where indicated, and you'll be taken to a new area where you can select whether to use the blog feed or comments link as the source of the RSS feed.

Your blog address will now be verified, and you'll be given the opportunity to change the title of your feed and its feed address if you would like. We recommend keeping it *as is* for the purposes of consistency and branding. Make a careful note of your feed address because you'll need it to subscribe to automatically send your blog feed to the pages of social networking applications (see Figure 9-7).

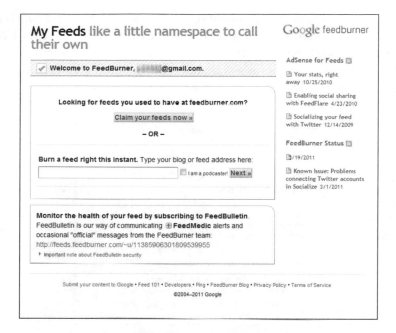

(Source: Feedburner.google.com)

Figure 9-6   FeedBurner offers one method to incorporate RSS feeds into your blog.

(Source: Feedburner.google.com)

Figure 9-7   FeedBurner now gives you the option to change the title and address of your feed.

FeedBurner also offers a variety of statistics to help you keep track of who is visiting your blog. We recommend you select both the **Clickthroughs** and the **I Want More** options (see Figure 9-8). These options provide additional ways to track reach and popularity of your posts as well as clickthroughs, which are additional members of your blog audience who have found you via their RSS feeds.

(Source: Feedburner.google.com)

Figure 9-8   The FeedBurner stats options provide an opportunity to track the popularity of your posts.

After you set the options for your RSS feed, you can start publicizing it via the platform options available through FeedBurner (see Figure 9-9).

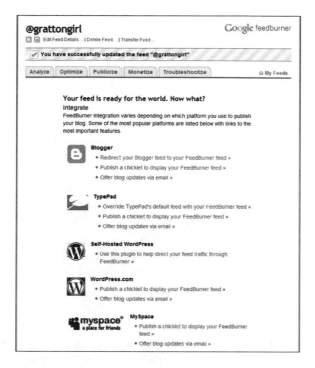

(Source: Feedburner.google.com)

Figure 9-9   Begin publicizing your feed through the platform options available on FeedBurner.

Tags and Tag Clouds

Tags are keywords or phrases that are used by search engines to locate your posts. They are basically "spider food" for the Web and are used to create traffic for your blog. Effective use of tags can dramatically increase the number of readers and, ultimately, subscribers to your blog. Choose those words that best describe the content of your blog posts as your tags. They are primarily listed at both the bottom of your posts and also in the Tag Cloud widget on your sidebar.

Popular tags usually show up as larger than their neighbors in a tag cloud, as illustrated in Figure 9-10.

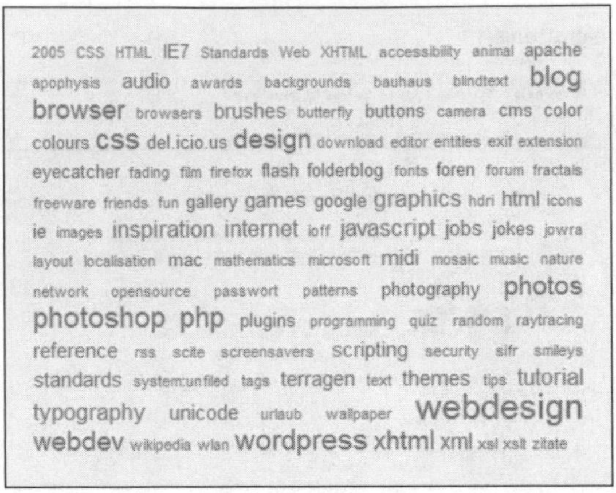

(Source: Jowra.com)

Figure 9-10   Examples of tag clouds; the most popular tags are shown as the largest in each cloud.

With Google Tag Clouds, you can create tags by either going to the Posts menu in the left sidebar and then selecting the Post Tags page or, after you've written a new post, selecting the Post Tags section on the right of the Add New Post page. The latter is more advantageous because you can use the post you just authored to search for the best tags within it.

Embedding a YouTube Video into Your Blog

Log on to your blog and go to your dashboard. Once there, click **Post** and create the post in which you choose to include your video by first typing out the text and adding a title. Then click the **HTML** tab to switch to HTML view. Make sure you choose the spot in your text where you want to insert the video.

In a new window, go to YouTube and locate the video you would like to insert into your blog. Under the video, click the **Share** button, and you'll see **Embed** appear as an option (see Figure 9-11).

Click **Embed**, and you'll see highlighted code in blue (shaded, as shown in Figure 9-12). Now you can copy this and paste it into the area you have designated within your blog. Save your post and click **Preview** to try it out before finally clicking **Publish**.

(Source: Youtube.com)

Figure 9-11   Clicking the **Share** button allows you to select the Embed option on YouTube.

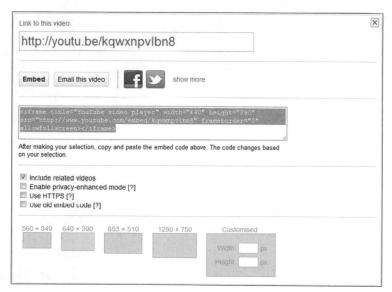

(Source: Youtube.com)

Figure 9-12   Clicking **Embed** highlights the code you need to insert into your blog.

You'll discover more advanced blogging tips and tricks later on in Parts III and IV of the book, where we also share some exclusive blogging secrets of the social media elite. Now that you know the basic mechanics of the various social media platforms, it's time to move on to our 10 steps to building a fast and effective online presence.

The 10-Step Method to Building a Fast and Effective Online Presence

10

Step 1: Listen First, Engage Second

Many define an interactive marketplace as a modern-day phenomenon, based on the uptake of social media marketing tools that have shifted the way marketers find and engage with their customers. But in fact, interactive marketplaces have been in existence for as long as communication itself. However, there has been a shift from direct, face-to-face transactions to the indirect interactions of the Internet that enable our businesses to span the globe and virtually manage thousands of accounts without needing to employ thousands of staff members.

Some will argue that this, too, is far from new. After all, interactive technology that allowed business to be conducted instantly, yet remotely, took off with the invention of the telephone. What has changed, and what is continuing to evolve with the help of online technology, is the consumer's relationship with a brand. The process is moving from a transaction-based effort to a conversation, where the customer has the ability to interrupt and modify a brand's message through new media intervention.

Monologue Versus Interactive Communication

A business or brand that communicates with its consumers purely through one-way media can be said to be employing monologue-based marketing, which probably won't be heard actively by its audience due to the fact that it's basically a business voice that's spouting a particular message such as "Buy this now," "Trend this," or "Click here to visit our site." It doesn't work and leaves today's respondents asking "Why should I?" The marketers have forgotten that promotion today begins and ends with building and sustaining trust. Interactive communications, on the other hand, take place when both sides pay attention to the other and a dialogue is struck between them. As with all forms of communication, the best dialogue happens when we listen to what the other party is saying before we respond. Don't be the first to dive in with your sales pitch. Instead, sit back, observe the market, and listen.

It's one of the most valuable tricks that anyone who wants to build a social media presence can master, and yet it's one of those practices that many businesses still choose to forget.

It's important to remember that social media is not about technology; it's about communication. The technology behind today's social media is just a mechanism that facilitates our exchange of ideas.

> Remember that the technology behind social media is just a mechanism that facilitates our exchange of ideas.

Learning How to Listen

So the first step to success in social media is listening. But how do we manage to tune in to millions of blogs, tweets, and messages and so on? "Surely there aren't enough hours in the day," we hear you cry!

It's actually easier than you might think. There are some wonderful listening and *Share of Voice* (SoV) tools and services out there that do all the trawling for you and find the snippets of information you need to pay attention to. There are many to choose from, some free and some available on a subscription fee basis. Here are some of the most popular and effective options to get you started.

Google Alerts

Google Alerts allows you to search for your brand or company name (or any competitors for that matter) to find out what is being said about you (or them). Just sign in to your Google account, go to google.com/alerts, and type in a search for your particular brand or company name (see Figure 10-1).

Select **Everything** as the type and **Once a day** or **As it happens** for how often. Finally, select the email address that you want the results delivered to. Now follow the same procedure for other keywords relating to your industry. You'll get an email once daily for each alert. Click the links and see what people are saying about you, your competitors, and your industry in general.

(Source: Google.com)

Figure 10-1   Google Alerts offers listening device options.

You'll no doubt need to refine your search terms based on the number of irrelevant links you get. For instance, a search for *candy apples* might yield lots of posts about fruit or even posts about people by the name of Candy. By adding quotation marks in the search term (*"candy apples"* rather than *candy apples*), you'll get far more relevant results.

Twitter Advanced Search

Twitter Search is a great tool for increasing your local customer base as well as checking out what the general buzz is about your industry. Over time, this tool enables you to build up your account with potential customers located nearby by using advanced search features, including geo-targeting. You can search by location as well as area of interest and focus on building relationships with those closest to you.

> Listening is the most important step to success in social media.

To get started, log in to Twitter's Advanced Search (see Figure 10-2) and start with some geo-targeted keyword searches. For example, if you're interested in finding people in New York who are into wine, you might search for the following: "wine bar" near: "New York city" within: "10 miles."

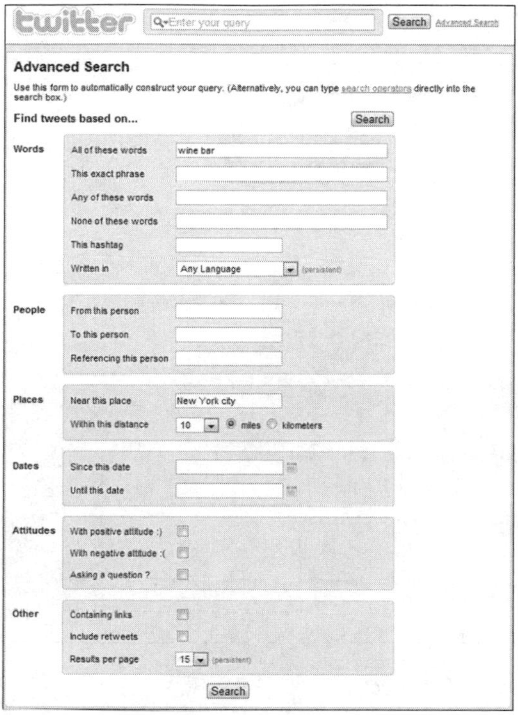

(Source: Twitter.com)

Figure 10-2   Twitter's Advanced Search options.

The results page will be filled with relevant potential followers (and competitors), giving you some insight into what people are both tweeting about and searching for (see Figure 10-3).

Experiment by trying out different combinations of keywords and search radii until you find the most relevant results for your business. You can then automate this process by subscribing to the search feed using *Really Simple Syndication* (RSS) as shown in Figure 10-4, which will enable you to view the results every day in your feed reader.

(Source: Twitter.com)

Figure 10-3   Example results found using Twitter's Advanced Search option.

(Source: Twitter.com)

Figure 10-4   Receive daily updates by clicking the RSS feed link: "Feed for this query."

Technorati

Technorati is a first-class blog search tool that helps you track keywords used in blogs and, once you start blogging yourself, allows you to keep an eye on any posts out there that are similar to yours (see Figure 10-5).

(Source: Technorati.com)

Figure 10-5   Technorati is the definitive blog search tool.

Technorati uses an easy interface. Each blog offers a link to an RSS feed, so you can easily track its entries as they are posted. Again, this provides an invaluable way to find the material others are posting and allows you to engage in a way that answers the questions being asked by your particular industry and, more importantly, its consumers.

It's important not to bombard yourself with too many tools. Stick with a few really good ones to keep you informed and updated. You might want to use a fee-based, all-in-one tool such as NutshellMail (Nutshellmail.com), shown in Figure 10-6. This monitors your brand on all the popular social media platforms, including LinkedIn, Facebook, Twitter, and YouTube. It may work out to be the best long-term solution for you, but we feel it's worthwhile to spend some time getting to know the individual free tools to familiarize yourself with the various search and RSS feed mechanisms.

(Source: Nutshellmail.com)

Figure 10-6 Paid search tools such as NutshellMail provide a comprehensive listening service that covers all major social media platforms.

Organizing Your Findings for Maximum Benefit

So you've been listening carefully and now your business has accumulated a steady stream of information pertaining to your industry sector in general. You have it! It's all there, but what exactly do you do with it, and how can you use it to help build an effective social media strategy?

Now it's time for Step 2: Understand and Build Your Social Media Voice.

11

Step 2: Understand and Build Your Social Media Voice

Understanding Share of Voice and Sentiment

To find your social media voice, you first need to clearly understand its impact within the social media spectrum and the emotions or sentiment that might be attached to it. All this can be tracked and is referred to in social media terms as your *Share of Voice* (SoV). It's the conversations going on about your brand versus your competitors or your business sector in general. Likewise, *sentiment* refers to the amount of emotion attached to each mention made. You can calculate and monitor both SoV and sentiment through the information gleaned by using the tools and services we introduced in step 1. If you do it right, over time your social media presence will grow, and as a result, so will your voice.

Calculating and Monitoring

When looking at all the mentions tracked by the listening tools you have chosen to employ, make sure you monitor those that are positive, negative, and neutral in a way that enables you to assign a weight to each category (for example Positive = 1, Neutral = 3 and Negative = 5) to calculate your average sentiment.

To find your SoV, you need to divide the number of conversations or mentions of your brand by the total number of conversations or mentions about other brands in your market.

By creating a spreadsheet template (see Figure 11-1), you'll be able to easily and clearly track your brand alongside your competitors. This provides a great way to see how your brand is finding its social media voice and growing in both share and positive sentiment month-by-month.

Over time, you'll be able to see exactly how your social interaction benefits your brand. This will enable you to make smarter and more confident marketing decisions. Above all, this step when employed long-term in your social media strategy, will allow you to keep in control of your social media platforms, to see which of them benefits your brand the most and which needs further effort to create an impact.

Creating a spreadsheet to display and monitor both SoV and sentiment is a great way to track your social media growth and to instill confidence in your social media team.

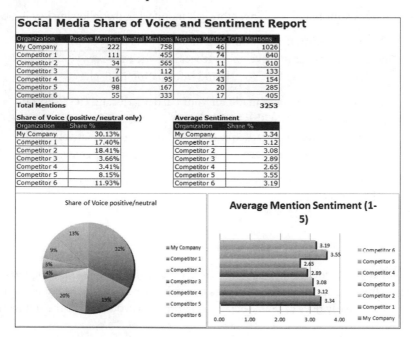

(Source: Convince & Convert LLC)

Figure 11-1   An example spreadsheet showing SoV and sentiment.

Building Awareness

People can't purchase your product or service if they don't know it exists, so you need to know how to build on your presence in a way that maximizes awareness of your brand. Creating brand awareness through traditional forms of media has always been a costly exercise, but today social media brings it within reach of even the smallest business.

After all, social media gives you easy access to literally millions of people across a huge geographic and multilingual area, in contrast to traditional media such as television, where only those within a limited geographic location who happen to be tuned in at the right time to "catch it" receive information. What's more, television allows for no interaction between the customer and the business[1], whereas you can engage freely with thousands of potential customers through social media, and the accessibility of messages and posts doesn't rely on the right-place, right-time factor.

Marketing via social media can easily go viral if produced and delivered in the right way. You will have often seen content on popular blogs with hundreds of *likes* and *retweets* that have been republished from much smaller sites. Being able to track how others are using and responding to your social media material is a powerful indicator that you are on the right track to substantially increasing your brand awareness.

You can track your brand awareness through monitoring the following key indicators:

- The amount of traffic and number of page views on your website; this indicates the resulting level of awareness for the messages you are sending out and the way that your brand information is displayed.

- The number of searches made for your particular brand (terms, products, and so on). Again, this highlights an awareness of your products or services within the marketplace and allows you to effectively track audience and consumer growth within your own brand arena.

- The number of video and other content views relating to your brand and business.

Signs of Engagement

Signs of engagement are the pointers that tell you which people are those most likely to buy your products and services through their interest in you and your brand. In the early days of your social media presence, you can use the following to

---

1. However, this is shifting with the gradual evolution of interactive television services, in addition to the delivery of such services, for example IPTV.

steer yourself toward the right kind of interactions by studying your competitors and like-minded businesses. Look for

- Facebook page and content *likes*

- The number of *shares*

- Retweets on a subject related to your business

- Ratings

- Mentions (positive, negative, neutral)

- Blog comments and subscriber numbers

Find Your Brand Evangelists

Many marketers are still under the impression that the majority of online comments made are bound to be bad ones. But as you'll discover from continuing to monitor and grow your SoV, nothing could be further from the truth. You'll learn that those who are most vocal about you are almost always your fans and potentially your brand evangelists, those who do much of the promotional work for you. So find them and use them to your advantage.

Spotting and Optimizing Trends

By spotting and optimizing trends correctly and frequently, you'll be able to identify trends before they happen and discover those keywords that will work to attract customers to your brand instead of to your competitors.

> Your brand voice and social voice are one and the same. Don't make the mistake of trying to separate them.

Look for trends and themes that come up repeatedly in your particular arena. Use them to provide discussion and value to readers and followers. They will arm you with great insight about how your industry's products or services fit into your consumers' lives. In addition, be sure to study the terminology used in discussions, noting any keywords that come up often because these will prove useful when optimizing your website and tagging future blog posts and other online content.

Brand Versus Social Voice: Making Them One and the Same

It shouldn't be a competition as to who shouts the loudest. Your brand and social voice should be one and the same: informative, responsive, and very, very approachable. With this in mind, your social media team, albeit made up of one or one hundred voices, needs to resonate a harmonious tone that over time will build trust and loyalty.

Traditional media experts still too often try to make a distinction between brand voice versus social voice, seeing the two as separate entities and failing to embrace the shift in communication that we have already come to understand from earlier chapters in this book. This shortsightedness can prove to be a death sentence to any brand looking to build a long-term effective social media presence.

The key lies in getting your social media team to work together in developing a voice that speaks for the business and brand as a whole. Clearly different posts by different people will vary in tone to some degree, but as mentioned previously, this is a harmony between a commonly bonded group of people with a specific message to tell. As time goes by, you will find specific members of your team best suited to specific social media areas. For example, Jane might fit well into those questions, comments, and general posts surrounding hardware issues of a particular product, whereas David may be better suited to issues related to customer service, and Kevin's forte might lie in posting photos of news, events, and competitions. Start as you mean to go on by identifying your team's individual strengths and passions and work with them to fine-tune your social voice into one beautiful harmony.

Think of your social media voice as being a harmony of those personalities in your team who best reflect your brand message.

12

Step 3: It's Who You Know—Finding and Attracting the Influencers

The next step to social media success is finding and attaching yourself to key influencers. If you get the respect of well-known social media voices behind you, you're already assured a strong following. But how do you know who the influencers are in social media, and after you find out, how do you hunt them down?

Let's get started by defining exactly what we mean by *influence* in social media terms.

All That Glitters Isn't Gold

You might think that the key influencers are the ones with the most followers, when in actual fact this isn't necessarily the case. The most popular people at the social media party won't usually carry the number of Twitter followers as celebrities do, but the followers they *do* have hang on every word they have to tweet or post, and if they say "jump" well...you get the idea.

What's more, if you were to peruse Twitter's Suggested Users list, you'd certainly find plenty of celebrities with huge follower counts who are of much less value to you than those with fewer followers (fewer movie star appearances, but more potential clout for your brand, which is what really matters).

After all, those big celebrity accounts are likely to have strictly defined agendas promoting their own content, and their interest in your business is consequently going to be extremely limited. For example, former U.S. vice-president Al Gore interacts very little with the wider audience through social media, posting only the occasional tweet or message and following only a few who are probably on his staff.

True influence involves true engagement.

We may well be selling ice to the Eskimos here, as it's common sense when you think about it. But it's all too easy to be seduced by the big celebrity names you'll come across on the likes of Twitter, Facebook, and YouTube, so it would be remiss of us not to steer you away from the glare of the glitter and on to more productive routes of influence.

What Makes an Influencer?

This is a somewhat tricky question because the best influencers in social media aren't necessarily the ones in front of the camera. Instead, they tend to be witty and creative types, those who revel in Cross Platform Promotion (CPP) and who have mastered the art of having many fingers in multiple media pies. They will have a substantial number of connections and followers (many of them also influential by association) but not so many as to become disconnected from their social media audiences.

Influencers tend to engage in conversation with random individuals and retweet/repost a variety of content simply because *they* find it interesting. They lead and create trends rather than just follow them. In other words, they truly engage and don't treat social media as a purely promotional device.

Influencers provide social media newbies with interesting content, clever responses, and a keen eye for new information to be seen and heard by those likeminded people who will follow. In turn, they may well be influenced by you as your social media personality grows and your voice becomes fine-tuned. After all, true influence involves both the influencer and the target audience. Influential engagement has a cyclic effect, as shown in Figure 12-1.

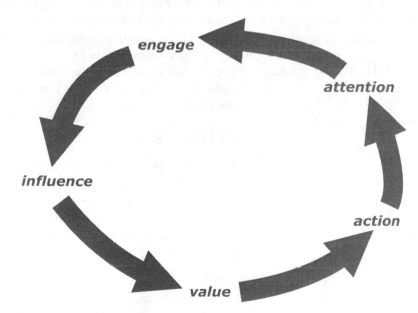

Figure 12-1   The cycle of influence.

So now that you know what makes an influencer in social media, how do you go about finding influencers?

Key Factors to Help You Identify Influencers Important to You

Finding those influencers who will be most beneficial to your social media success begins with understanding the facets that detirmine their level of influence. With this in mind, we've put together a list of the attributes you need to look out for in order to find the right influencers for your brand.

Credibility

An influencer is first and foremost acknowledged as a leader or expert in his or her particular field. No one is knowledgeable about everything, however, so consider who the leading voices in your business sector are. If you already know their names, your core audience will too. For example, in the wireless technology sector, the name Dean Anthony Gratton has become synonymous with Bluetooth and the knowledge and expertise surrounding it.

Frequency

Study how these people work with social media. Are they acknowledging and posting on a daily or weekly basis? Anything less frequent and they are unlikely to be highly influential in social media terms. You'll see a pattern emerging between the most influential users, defined by the fact that there is a high amount of interaction between them and their followers. In other words, they know how to keep their audience interested.

> Find out who your industry sector leaders are on each platform and engage with them.

Platform Leaders

Platform leaders are active, subject-led engagers who choose to focus on their particular area of expertise in a prominent manner, on a particular social media platform. This doesn't mean that other platforms are excluded from their social media strategy, however, and many choose to utilize CPP.

It's important to find out who's leading your industry sector on each platform and to engage with them.

Klout Score

Klout (Klout.com) is acknowledged as a great online tool for measuring, analyzing, and monitoring influence in social media. Primarily tied in to Twitter activity, it has now extended its assessment to Facebook and is preparing to integrate LinkedIn engagement, too. Klout scores range from 1 to 100, with higher scores representing the strongest influencers (see Figure 12-2). The team behind Klout claims to use "over 35 variables on Facebook and Twitter to measure True Reach, Amplification Probability, and Network Score."

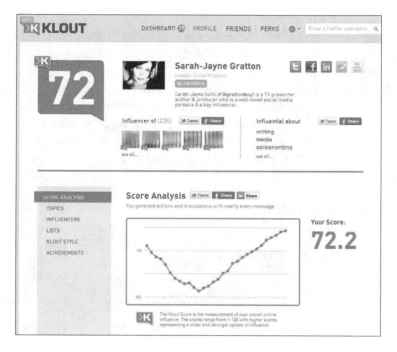

(Source: Klout.com)

Figure 12-2   Klout analyzes your social media activity and provides a score based on your overall online influence.

Klout describes *True Reach* as "the size of your engaged audience and is based on those of your followers and friends who actively listen and react to your messages." Your *Amplification* score is said to be "the likelihood that your messages will generate actions (retweets, @messages, likes, and comments) and is on a scale of 1 to 100, and your *Network* score indicates how influential your engaged audience is and is also on a scale from 1 to 100."

Your Klout score is highly correlated to clicks, comments, and retweets and is another useful way to monitor your own growing influence in social media and to find those all-important key influencers. A Klout score of 60 and above is an excellent indicator of strong online influence.

Peer Index

Another identifier of online influence is PeerIndex (Peerindex.net), which provides a 1 to 100 scoring index, similar to Klout, but focusing on the monitoring and analysis of *social capital* (a measure of a person or a brand's reputation within social media). PeerIndex defines their scoring system as giving "a relative measure of your online authority."

PeerIndex scores reflect both the impact of your social media activity and the reputation you have gained as a result of what they call your "reputational capital on the Web" along with your "authority fingerprint." This fingerprint is based on eight benchmark topics built on category-based levels to include audience, authority, topic resonance, activity, and realness, which is an interesting metric that, like Klout, indicates a person's or brand's social media influence. A score of 60 or more indicates a high level of social media influence. You can see an example of @grattonboy's PeerIndex analysis and ranking in Figure 12-3.

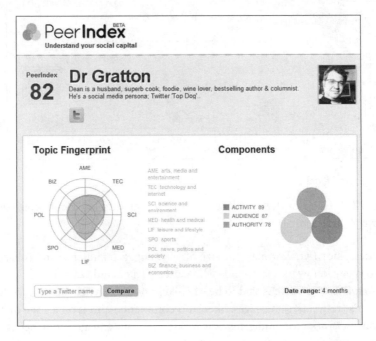

(Source: Peerindex.com)

Figure 12-3   PeerIndex is another great way to assess both your and potential followers reputational capital and social media influence.

More recently, PeerIndex has linked Facebook and LinkedIn accounts to give a
more complete picture of social media presence and influence.

A Valuable Audience Awaits

Engaging the influencers in your business sector enables you to engage *their* audience, and, as with the influencer, their value to you is based on a number of factors.
These are timing, relationships, and enthusiasts.

Timing

Is it the right time and the right place to connect? First, consider whether your chosen influencers are ahead of the field. Do they, for example, retweet from obscure
and unique sources regularly? Keep in mind that if an audience isn't getting useful
information when they need it or receiving secondhand news, they might well tune
it out. As mentioned numerous times, it pays to research and keep ahead of the rest
in terms of content. Make sure that your chosen influencers are timing their tweets
and posts to keep abreast of current issues that are relevant and beneficial to your
business and brand.

Relationships

Given the previous point, think about how closely the audience is related to the
influencer and how much they use the information received from them. Bear in
mind that a firsthand tweet can reach us in an instant. Secondhand information
takes longer. (Consider an article on a blog posted to Facebook and then
retweeted...you get the idea.) So, again, it pays to find the relationship between all
that's fresh and unique in your sector and to then connect to the transmitters of
that information.

Enthusiasts Rather Than Celebrities

As mentioned earlier in this chapter, people follow because they're keen to find out
specific information and to form relationships. In business terms, this means engaging with hobbyists and enthusiasts who are knowledgeable and real. The celebrity
appeal of the big names probably won't reward you with an effective following, so
as already discussed, don't be fooled by the gloss and instead focus on the real influencers, whose followers are assured of a relevant stream of information that adds
continual value.

Attracting Engagement for Long-Term Social Media Success

Finding those people with the characteristics laid out in this chapter and attracting their engagement is fundamental to your long-term social media success. The utilizing and provision of fresh information that continually adds value will assure you of their support in spreading the word about your brand through their sustained influence.

What's more, you'll be starting your journey to becoming a key social media influencer yourself!

13

Step 4: Don't Get Too Big for Your Social Media Boots!

As you become involved in the social media scene, you'll almost certainly encounter what has been coined as social media narcissism. It's derived from what is more commonly termed Narcissistic Personality Disorder (NPD) described by the psychiatrists' Diagnostic and Statistical Manual of Mental Disorders (or DSM) as "a pervasive pattern of grandiosity, need for admiration, and a lack of empathy."

Narcissists (NPD people) have a "big personality" that is excessively preoccupied with personal adequacy, power, and prestige. Everyone has *some* need for attention, but NPD people are pathologically obsessed with it, and for many, social media is the perfect breeding ground for them. Recognition and awareness of this destructive, yet common disorder in the social media scene can save you intense pain and grief.

Throughout history, the rich and powerful among us have chosen to document their status through portraiture, with the help of the great artists who, in turn, have had their own portraits hung in the same galleries and museums. It's a bid for immortality, if you like, a way to capture greatness for all to see. After all, we all strive to be noticed and remembered.

Today's self-portraits are the digital kind, online representations of the people we want to be. They are created with pixels, tweets, and posts in favor of paint. They offer opportunities for self-expression but can all too easily display egotism and self-absorption.

It happens to us all; that point of complete self-assurance where the *self* becomes more important than the *assurance*, and make no mistake, it will happen to your business on the way to becoming one of the social media elite. It will sneak up on you unexpectedly like a thief in the night. One minute you're tweeting about the importance of listening to your customers and of the virtues of gratitude in customer service and the next you're retweeted to the point of becoming the next Messiah. Be warned! This is your red light, your signal to *stop* and take stock of what is happening.

You see, it's all too easy to be seduced by the responses and comments surrounding that latest and greatest post. Be flattered and honored, but don't allow the adulation to distract you. Remain focused and bear in mind that you're only as good as your latest post, so continue to ensure that each new one is as good or better than the one before.

It's not always about the "stun them with knowledge factor" either; social media success hinges on response and conversation, remember? A two-way stream. Sure, you want to make an impact and impart value as much as possible while giving your posts and tweets

Pay particular attention to any negative feedback because this can prove to be the most valuable of all.

the *wow* factor, but you need to stay connected and in touch with your followers and subscribers and to make them feel as special as they make *you* feel with their positive feedback and acclaim.

And remember to pay especial attention to the negative feedback. Don't sweep it under the rug with a "what do they know" click of your mouse. These are the comments that can prove the most valuable to your business and your social media longevity.

Dealing with Social Media Narcissists

It's important to remember when dealing with social media narcissists that their personas are shallow and volatile. They may be your allies one moment and bitter enemies the next. You can recognize them by their inability (or refusal) to empathize and their single-voice or monotone postings, where any criticism is immediately deleted and its posters blocked. Generally, narcissists demand loyalty and ego stroking. If you choose to get involved in their world, be prepared to perpetually walk on eggshells and to keep your true feelings masked, no matter how disgusting or annoying the person's behaviors are. Never criticize them unless you are willing to go on their permanent black list.

When you've spotted those social media narcissists, it's best to steer well clear of them or be prepared to walk on eggshells for fear of being put on their black lists.

If you don't need or want anything from the social media narcissist, it's best to be cordial and distant from them. Keep firm boundaries. *Stay far away* and don't allow you or your team to be drawn into their charismatic web of illusion. If they choose to attack you, remember that you don't have to attack back. Participating in the world of the narcissist will undoubtedly only cause you setbacks and misery on your road to social media success.

14

Step 5: Instilling a Sense of Community

You've now laid your foundations, and it's time to start building your unique online community. Consider your blog posts, which, with the help of Chapter 8, "Blogging Your Way to Business Success," and Chapter 9, "The Secrets to a Successful Blog," you should have now sketched out and entered into your social media editorial calendar for review. They should all foster a community of like-minded readers who are looking for online kindred spirits and leaders who can impart knowledge in a way that will assist them and add value to their lives. If you read through your editorial calendar and discover that your proposed posts fall short of this in some way, it's time to go back to the drawing board in terms of content or, at least, to revise what you have laid down.

When you're happy with your planned posts, the key to start instilling a community-focused ethos is to spend time building relationships that not only engage with site users but also get them to interact with each other. After all, visitors need to know that they are part of an online community who's listening and who will respond and engage with them. Visitors are not likely to participate if they perceive that their comments and contributions are falling into some huge black online hole from which they will never be seen or referred to again.

Another problem can arise if none of your visitors are willing to be the first to comment and everyone waits for other comments to come in before adding their own. It's like being the first person to ask a question at a conference. Many prefer to wait until someone else opens up the floor for them. A good way to overcome this is to start the ball rolling with comments from colleagues and friends. Then, after the comments *do* come in, be sure to respond to them promptly and, where possible, refer or cross-reference their remarks to other comments received, which invites engagement between the two (or more) commenters. If someone leaves a great comment, be sure to mention it, or you could even create a new blog post around it.

Remember that it takes time to build trust within a community, and the trust you do forge can be easily lost. With this in mind, ensure that your team maintains a constant dialogue with your community. The effort spent in keeping members updated can prove valuable in other ways beyond building trust in your brand. The social media platforms you build are ideal for informing your community about website changes or new products or services.

> Ensure that your team maintains a constant dialogue with your community.

Content Curation

Using initial posts from those you know is an easy and effective way of getting your blog engine started, but once you start attracting comments and information from other sources, you need to think about curating this in a way that ensures a maximum return on your online community investment. Weeding out the strong content from the chaff rewards your contributors with continued value, and by involving your key influencers through the resonance and echoing of their comments, your posts will sustain their interest and intensity. Effective content curation will bring in new members to the community who will see it as a great place to comment and be heard. Content can come from a number of sources, and it's up to you to identify the best ones in terms of industry and community relevance. After you have refined your content, you can organize and share it with your community in a way that generates comments and contributions.

Your team should work to reward contributing visitors and members early on, either through a quick response or a lengthier note of gratitude for all to see. Where possible, set up your comment system to use screen names and avatars as part of a response so that those searching can quickly identify themselves within your posts. If someone leaves a particularly thoughtful or useful comment, be sure to keep his or her username on file in a private list with a brief note about their comment. If a related thread comes around at a later date, you can then refer back to your list and ask for that individual's specific comments. It's a great way to reward and build a community that looks to continually support and engage with you.

Your Online Focus Group

Also consider putting your community to work as a focus group to recommend positive enhancements to your business and brand. Don't make the mistake of thinking that your social media community need be confined to your blog. The Indian airline, Jet Airways, has built a Facebook community (facebook.com/jetairways) that provides guests with real-time news, updates about flight schedules, new customer programs, route additions, services, and special offers. It also provides guests with an online forum to discuss their experiences (see Figure 14-1).

(Source: Facebook.com/jetairways)

Figure 14-1 Jet Airways became one of the first Asian carriers to form a successful online community via Facebook.

In addition to Facebook, Jet Airways created an online community on Twitter (twitter.com/jetairways) to actively engage with its customers and major stakeholders and to provide another channel to monitor and enhance the Jet Airways travel experience.

Discovering the Nerve Center of Your Community

There are a lot of platforms available that you can choose to use to build a strong community. However, there are only so many hours in the day, and even though we show you how to use *Cross Platform Promotion* (CPP) later in this book to time-manage your team's social media efforts, remember that every good community needs one nerve center—a hub of operations, if you like—from which everything else extends out and becomes connected.

Most experts agree that your social media community should begin with your blog, the reason being primarily that this is where most search engines will lead to, and it's a place where you are unrestricted by word count and themes as with Twitter or Facebook. Many choose to use their blogs as a base station or hub, from which their brand messages are echoed out across the other platforms and followers are funneled back to the primary hub. However, this is a not a hard-and-fast rule, and if you find that the majority of your interaction takes place on Twitter or Facebook, it might make sense to focus on one or the other as the nerve center of your community.

Let It Develop Its Own Personality

Social media can help your business or brand make connections to people and groups you might never encounter otherwise. Similarly, it can help you access other people's views and worlds in the same way that they can access yours. Over time, all of this connecting and embracing differences and viewpoints will create a unique community that forms its own personality.

It can be hard for some business leaders who are used to being in control and setting the tone of an organization to see a community they helped to establish as an independent body with its own personality and unique voice. But for a community to be all that it can be, those at its heart must be willing to embrace and support its individuality.

It's not about letting go of ethics and morals, but about allowing a community to evolve freely. Remember that a social community is formed from the public rather than peers or employees. With this in mind, be prepared to be flexible in terms of content in a way that shows you care about your members' views and are happy to celebrate them. Embrace user-generated content topics and give your members a sense of empowerment. Doing so will keep them loyal and ensure that the community remains fresh and continues to grow in a way that, long-term, will prove valuable for your business.

The effectiveness of your community building can be measured by monitoring increases and decreases in following, keeping track of email lists, *Really Simple Syndication* (RSS) subscribers, and by measuring conversion rates for your site; that is, the number of casual visits to a website compared to the number of those people who buy a product or make a similar action. Also keep track of interactions, types of engagement such as comments, follow-on post links, and their outcomes in terms of new subscribers and customers. This is a good step toward understanding your online community and giving them what they want.

15

Step 6: Do You Need a Brand Makeover?

"Reinvention allows us to continually discover new gifts within ourselves."

—Sarah-Jayne Gratton

Why Change Is Necessary

Like everything in life, we tend to construct our own psychological safety nets for both our businesses and ourselves. These generally surface in the way that we present and express brand *us* to others (we like to call them communication *armor*), and they can be incredibly difficult to break free of. They also occur in social media, where, over time, we can become staid and repetitive.

Sometimes the best way forward is to stop going forward altogether and, instead, to take a step to the side to re-evaluate how best to break through this communication armor. In social media terms, this means re-evaluating our content and other presentation elements such as page design on a regular basis.

"Review and renew!" Make this your mantra and be sure that your brand ambassadors do too.

We all have a vision of where we want our social media roadmap to take us, but all too often, instead of embracing the track ahead, we find ourselves retracing our old footsteps over and over and making the same mistakes. This is where so many businesses fail in their use of social media, and it's one of the most important lessons your business can learn.

The rule to long-term social media success is this: Review and renew! Make it your mantra, and be sure that your brand ambassadors do too.

Embracing Change in Social Media

As you will have learned by now, social media has and will continue to dramatically change the way we promote our businesses and ourselves. It has opened many new doors through building engaging relationships with customers by replacing monologue with interactive, two-way conversations, as discussed in Chapter 10, "Step 1: Listen First, Engage Second."

Social media *is* change. It is a change that we all are learning, but yet some are resistant to it, predominantly out of fear that the consumer will suddenly have control over their brand message. The paradox is that by utilizing the power of the consumer, we are creating an army of brand ambassadors working globally to promote us, which is a blessing rather than a curse, as long as we continue to engage and provide a high-level of positive interaction and as long as we ensure that any issues with our products or services are resolved quickly. Resolutions to problems are often the best form of promotion, and they work to turn low-voltage negatives into 1000w positives, so long as we don't take our eyes off the ball.

Keeping It Fresh

As the old saying goes, "You never get a second chance to make a first impression," and your social media platforms are no exception. To ensure that all of them continue to make a positive impression, you need to keep them well maintained and give them the occasional makeover.

Make sure that your brand message is always up-to-par by following the steps outlined in the following sections.

Keep Your Keywords and Tags Up-to-Date

Keywords and tags are the building blocks of effective optimization for your website and blog and are the tools that make it possible for others to easily find you. It is important to revisit this list at least once a quarter to cut out any superfluous terms and to add in new ones that focus upon fresh content that is highly relevant to your products or services. Make use of online tools such as WordTracker (Wordtracker.com) and Google AdWords Keywords Tool (adwords.google.com) to expand your current keyword set and obtain information about relevance and search volume. After you have identified the tags and keywords that will bring in the highest traffic in relation to your products and services, incorporate these into your blog and website to create maximum exposure of your brand.

Keep Your Copy Fresh

Stale and outdated content can be unattractive for both visitors and search engines. In fact, search engines often reward sites for having content that is fresh and frequently updated by promoting them up the list. When writing new content for your blog, try to include the primary keyword phrase approximately five times. And don't forget that including the phrase in your hyperlink and metadata are great ways to strengthen your post's relevancy for search. This task should be tackled at least once a quarter after you update your keyword list.

Update Your Profiles

As with your copy, spend time every few months updating your profiles on all of your social media platforms to incorporate any important company news and to include any upcoming events, products, or services. Change your product photos regularly to keep them fresh and appealing and always ensure that team photos are regularly updated to, again, keep them current and clickable. It's also a great opportunity to get your brand ambassadors together for fun, social sessions.

> Regularly check your hyperlink to make sure that they take your visitors where they need to go.

Rediscover Your Relevance with an Online Search

A great way to ensure that old, irrelevant information is removed and that potential customers, followers, and subscribers are finding your latest content is by performing a search on Google (or other search engine) for your business on a monthly basis to monitor where your content is being listed. If you have updated your tags and keywords correctly, your listings should appear in their most relevant form first, but bear in mind that you might not be at the very top of any keyword search result list if you haven't paid for a premium listing. Likewise, bear in mind that it may take up to ten weeks for your content to be indexed by the various search engines. Your domain host may be able to offer additional *Search Engine Optimization* (SEO) tools/services to further boost your ranking.

Once you find them, be sure to follow any links through to make certain that you take your visitors to where they need to go. Fix any broken links along the way because these not only have usability implications, but can also negatively affect your brand by creating a poor user experience, especially when they reference old articles that have been taken down or products that no longer exist.

Don't Be Afraid to Try Something New

Social media platforms are continually changing and evolving, and many offer their users the opportunity to try out beta features, widgets, and tools on a regular basis before their general release. Let your platforms know you are keen to grow and

Your domain host may be able to offer SEO tools or services to boost your ranking.

expand your social media application, and don't be afraid to jump onboard and discover new ways that social media can work to assist your business.

Be Your Own Traffic Cop

You probably look at your analytics on a monthly basis to understand where your external traffic is coming from. But take some time to also look for patterns or anomalies in your data. For instance, if you notice that important high-level or product website pages or blogs aren't performing as you would like, try altering the variables on the page, such as content and call to action, which we discuss further in Chapter 18, "Step 9: Social Media Darwinism—Survival of the Fittest."

Be the Change You Wish to See

Embracing change in social media through continually pushing forward our boundaries with new content, widget integration, and the clever application of analytics will set us apart as leaders of our platforms.

Remember that social media is a change that we are all still learning to embrace through our relationships with each other. Accept the change and learn from it to grow both you and your business.

16

Step 7: Become a Social Conductor

So, What Is a Social Conductor, Exactly?

A social conductor is a brand ambassador who knows how to leverage the power of social media through *Cross Platform Promotion* (CPP)—as we introduce in Chapter 17, "Step 8: Introducing Cross Platform Promotion"—and the use of social media tools to build a structure of social media integration that unites the various platforms to unify a brand message.

In essence, we can look upon a social conductor as the conductor of an orchestra, ensuring that each instrument being played comes together at the right time and with the right intensity to create the perfect symphony.

How to Conduct Your Social Media Traffic

Now that you've set up your platforms and are learning the tricks that will set you apart from the competition, it's time to fully maximize the traffic you receive to ensure that all your hard work is viewed and appreciated by as many potential customers as possible.

A social conductor is a brand ambassador who knows how to leverage the power of social media through CPP and the use of social media tools.

A great way to help you achieve this is to use traffic-boosting tools such as those provided by Digg (Digg.com) and StumbleUpon (Stumbleupon.com). Also known as *submit tools*, there are hundreds of different options out there, and positioning them correctly will enable you to become a true social conductor. Unfortunately, none of us have the time to be an active member on more than just a few social media sites, and trying to target too many of them by adding countless buttons and widgets to your blog will only make it cluttered and ineffective. So be selective in your choices and stick with the tools that have the most clout and which we talk about in this chapter.

Traffic-boosting tools such as Digg and StumbleUpon enable you to become a true social conductor by maximizing the traffic you receive to your website, blog, and other social media platforms.

Among social media sites, there are a huge variety of audiences, types of content that's popular, amount of traffic that's sent to popular links, and so on. Most experts in social media agree that the quality to traffic of your platforms is more important than the quantity. In terms of linking from your blog, the quality of traffic that you receive from social media will largely depend upon finding the right fit in terms of the tools you employ on your blog to direct your readers to your other social media platforms and entice them to spread the word about posts they have enjoyed. So experiment with a few and find out what works best for you.

The Five Elements That Make a Great Social Conductor

The conductor model as defined by Jay Deragon in 2010 leverages five elements of interaction with the marketplace, and we discuss each of these individually in the following sections.

Attention

Great social conductors do things that create attention from the marketplace. However, the things they do draw attention to people's ideas, wants, desires, and needs rather than direct attention to themselves. They build social capital by doing things that people can participate in and benefit from. They provide content that is in context to people's intentions rather than the intentions of their organization. For example, the *Pepsi Refresh* social media campaign (Refresheverything.com) has given millions of dollars in grant money to fund projects in six categories: health, arts and culture, food and shelter, the planet, neighborhoods, and education. The campaign has resulted in it conducting thousands of new visitors to its Facebook page and its blog, which have translated into many new customers for the brand.

The Pepsi campaign continues to draw the right attention, not just for one event, but works to conduct traffic 24/7 and 365 days of the year (see Figure 16-1).

> Social conductors build social capital by doing things that people can participate in and benefit from.

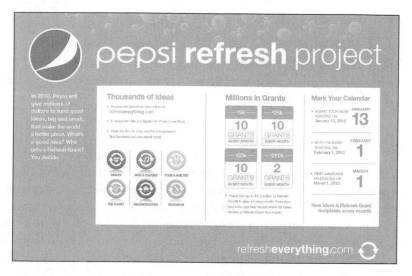

(Source: Refresheverything.com)

Figure 16-1   The Pepsi Refresh project continues to conduct traffic a year following its conception.

Awareness

Social conductors draw attention to people and things that are social. Such things could be anything that people desire, want, or need; the conductor enables people to easily access information that is in alignment with their intents. By raising awareness of issues that are important and relevant to society, conductors are in fact raising awareness of their brands. Mainstream media and the participants are likely to discuss the Pepsi campaign mentioned earlier, and the blogosphere will explode with commentary surrounding it for a long time to come.

Affinity

Social conductors create affinities in people by enabling them to interact, support, and communicate relevant information that is important to their wants, needs, desires, and intentions. By creating such affinities, social conductors are indirectly creating an affinity to themselves for the value created by the experience and interaction they enable.

Audience

By creating attention, awareness, and affinity, social conductors build an audience who relates to the actions, intents, and values created on their behalf.

Call to Action

The social conductor enables people to *act* on their desires, wants, needs, and intentions to become the enabler of action on behalf of the audience. As a result of being the enabler, confidence in the conductor grows; something that every brand and individual aspires to accomplish.

Campaigning for Votes

Some traffic-boosting sites, such as Digg, display a post's or link's popularity through the number of reader votes and views it receives. It can take well over 500 votes for yours to make it to the front page, whereas smaller alternatives such as Sphinn (Sphinn.com) might require many fewer views to take your posts to the top of the list. Obviously, larger sites like Digg tend to have more users, so in some ways it can be easier to get those all important views and votes. Still, this is something that you should consider as part of your social architecture.

Traffic-boosting sites will also provide widgets and plugins that you can embed into your blog, which allow users to vote for their favorite posts. Your blog software will also have widgets available, allowing you to share your posts to a variety of other platforms and sites.

Employ an Influencer

Some traffic-boosting sites, especially Digg, are impacted by who submits the link. Certain "power users" have hundreds or thousands of friends who follow their submissions and vote them up. So the profile of the submitter can play a large role in the success of the submission, and it can be hugely beneficial to find influential users to submit your content on a regular basis.

Find out who's popular on the traffic-boosting sites in your particular sector by doing a search for those topics where your posts might best sit, and then make a note of the submitters' names who come out on top again and again. These are the influencers you need to integrate into your connections.

How Long Will the Traffic Last?

Social media submit sites are notorious for sending a quick rush of traffic and then nothing at all. With most social media submit sites, popularity doesn't last long. StumbleUpon is one of the few exceptions. With StumbleUpon, you can still be getting trickles of traffic for several months or longer. You should additionally continue to rework your stories, posts, and links to regenerate interest and conduct continued traffic to your platforms.

Using these techniques to socially conduct your platforms will enable you to blend your online content into one perfectly polished symphony that will maintain its appeal for your audience.

> It can be extremely valuable to connect and even employ the power users and key influencers on traffic-boosting sites to drive traffic to you by posting your news and links.

17

Step 8: Introducing Cross Platform Promotion

"Cross Platform Promotion (or CPP) defines the synergetic partnership between social media platforms to bring about the greatest content exposure."
—Gratton & Gratton

A Synergetic Way of Thinking

When we first started talking about *Cross Platform Promotion* (CPP) early in 2010, there was a great deal of debate taking place about the best way for small businesses to promote themselves online. We attended a huge number of seminars with experts talking about the best platforms out there on which to make the strongest impact and very little about harnessing the overall power of the promotional options available.

> CPP enables you to leverage your brand across the various social media platforms.

When it comes to building a brand, we've always believed in the power of teamwork, each member of the team working together to spread the message quickly and with as much impact as possible so as to maximize *Return on Investment* (ROI). In the same way, those with the most effective social media presence were utilizing the power of their various platforms to work as a united team in spreading their message, and this is where the term CPP began to come into focus for us. CPP isn't a new concept (far from it, in fact). Consider a television advertisement that refers to a newspaper coupon that links to an in-store promotion that refers back to the television and newspaper campaigns that are picked up by the local radio stations as part of the promotion and you start to get the picture. The trouble with these earlier forms of traditional CPP is that they quite often relied on huge financial outlay to bring them into the public domain in an effective way. This historically created a corporate class system where advertorial clout was governed by wealth.

Social media has changed all that by allowing creativity rather than finances to shine online and become viral, creating a wave of interest and *pull* that was previously inaccessible to the masses. By learning how to leverage yourself and your brand across the platforms, you learn to truly grasp the power of social media.

Start with Your Strategy

If your business is truly going to get the most out of social media by engaging in a way that adds value to your brand and to others, it needs to have a cohesive strategy. By now you should have a much stronger knowledge of how social media is going to work for you, and a strategy, if not already formulated, should be well on its way to completion. You'll also have your key platforms in mind, which you'll have chosen confidently as the ones that will work best for your business.

Now comes the task of ensuring that consistent messaging is spread across all your platforms and that there is regularity to your posts. Think of using CPP in the same way you would your traditional marketing efforts but without the hefty associated price tag, and you'll immediately see the benefits. In the same way that you wouldn't expect to place an advertisement or advertorial piece in just one magazine and see sales rocket, you can't expect to put all your eggs into one social media platform basket. Taking your brand message viral in social media can be practically cost free, but it does require the clever use of your available channels and a well-executed approach. You need to start with a *core element* for all CPP activities, such as a new blog post, comment, website change, or video. Figure 17-1 gives an example of how this might work with a new blog post as the core element.

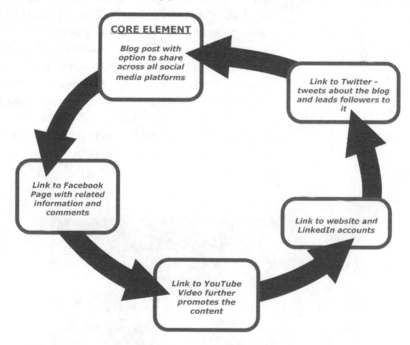

Figure 17-1   An example of CPP with a blog post as its core element.

Advertise Without Advertising

We've already shown how the best results in social media come from engaging in a two-way conversation. It's important to tie in your blog posts to matters that your subscribers and followers are eager to learn more about and to build them into conversations that are already taking place across your platforms. This clever trick enables you to stay on top of the trends taking place and will help to establish you as a trusted source of information and advice in your particular sector (see Figure 17-2).

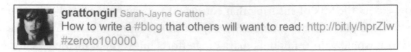

grattongirl Sarah-Jayne Gratton
How to write a #blog that others will want to read: http://bit.ly/hprZlw
#zeroto100000

Figure 17-2   Sarah-Jayne (a.k.a. @grattongirl) uses her followers' interest in blogging techniques to lead them to her own.

Sites such as Hootsuite and TweetDeck allow you to put all your social media accounts into one central location.

Time-Saving CPP Tools

Keeping a consistent message and presence across multiple social media sites can be time-consuming. That's where tools such as Hootsuite (Hootsuite.com) and TweetDeck (Tweetdeck.com) really come into their own, enabling you to put all your social media accounts into one central location. The software also enables easy CPP by allowing you to send updates to many of your platforms simultaneously, making it that much easier to manage several accounts at once and maintain consistency. There is also another very useful feature to schedule tweets and both Facebook and LinkedIn posts so that you can maintain a constant presence (see Figure17-3).

(Source: Tweetdeck.com)

Figure 17-3   TweetDeck is a Twitter-focused client that offers great CPP features, including scheduled updates.

Planning a CPP Schedule for Success

If used correctly, CPP can be your best social media friend. It's a great way to ensure that your message spreads across all your chosen social media platforms and reaches the greatest possible audience. Build it in to your social media strategy by using a schedule of where and when you will be most effective across various platforms and don't be afraid to reschedule several times during the course of a day to reach potential customers on different time zones. Table 17-1 shows an example of a CPP social media schedule.

Table 17-1   How CPP Might Be Used in a Daily Schedule

Time	Content	Audience
8 am/12pm/4pm	Morning greeting and noteworthy news of interest (CPP).	
11am/3pm/7pm	Retweets/replies (Twitter)	
	Links to blogs, posts, and videos of interest (CPP)	Local time/remote time/cross continental
2pm/6pm/10pm	Retweets/replies (Twitter)	
	Humor spot (CPP) related to your business or quirky memorable quote	
	Links to blogs, posts, and videos of interest (CPP)	

Using CPP to Create a Response Buzz

Effective use of CPP means getting the most out of the idiosyncrasies of each social media platform you choose to employ. For example, you might offer additional incentives for those people who like a particular Facebook page or tweet about their favorite product from your range with a link to a photo they have taken of it in their homes. You can also build in a geographically tagged response buzz through both Facebook and Foursquare (which we introduced in Chapter 7, "Foursquare: Putting Your Brand on the Map") by providing additional incentives based on location to a store or office where visitors might purchase your goods or services or, in the case of Foursquare, might be offered a badge based on the number of visits to your business or products they have purchased and provided tips for.

Again, CPP enables these customer mentions and accolades to echo their "loyalty" and reinforce the likelihood of future purchases.

CPP isn't new, but it has entered a brave new world of social media, where it will evolve alongside the platforms themselves to provide you with countless opportunities for creative brand promotion.

18

Step 9: Social Media Darwinism— Survival of the Fittest

In a 2010 Booz & Co. report on the marketing media ecosystem,[1] five key behaviors were identified that the social media fittest will possess in order to survive. We expand on them here to provide you with a valuable reference on which to measure your efforts and refer back to in order to secure the longevity of your social media success.

1. http://www.booz.com/global/home/what_we_do/services/marketing/42058081/MME

Shifting Customer Service into Social Media

This first finding is hardly a surprise, but it's one of the areas where so many businesses may get it wrong in social media. Throughout the book, we've reinforced how your social media presence needs to be one that continually activates consumers, engaging them in such a way that they feel motivated to respond and subsequently echo your message across their own social media networks, becoming your brand-advocates in the process.

Social media accelerates and democratizes publication, which means consumers can create content about your organization, and their influence is continuing to grow. According to a study carried out by NASDAQ group Right Now (Rightnow. com), an individual comment or post on a social media site carries greater influence today than similar comments in the past. This significant change represents the biggest challenge for customer service departments and staff. Instead of monitoring a limited number of broadcast channels, managers must recognize that *everyone* is empowered to publish. This can actually be a blessing in terms of workload because creative collaboration, where customers address each other's questions through social media, can reduce the burden on call centers and departments immensely—again, the customers themselves have trusted sources of information about your services and products.

Remember that your customer service staff must tap into the wisdom of crowds and experts in these communities to deliver better experiences to customers and continue the positive endorsements being echoed across your social media channels. Listening devices such as those we covered in Chapter 10, "Step 1: Listen First, Engage Second," will enable you to track, report, and provide feedback to consumers, to continually refresh your knowledge of their requirements, and to provide new and relevant social media content.

> Your customer service team can tap into the wisdom of your online communities to deliver better customer experiences.

Offering Cross Platform Choice

Customers expect consistency of message across your platforms, and they want options. No matter where they are, or what time it is, if you want to keep them happy, you need to offer multiplatform options that provide value to them when they need it.

The best way to provide consistent information across channels is to employ *Cross Platform Promotion* (CPP), as discussed in Chapter 17, "Step 8: Introducing Cross Platform Promotion," because many customers like to jump between platforms when trying to resolve an issue. A request that starts by searching your blog may lead to a discussion on your Facebook page, which could escalate to a call to action.

And it's important to remember that customers shouldn't *have* to act as the glue between your platforms, although of course they undoubtedly will if you employ an effective CPP strategy. A multichannel customer experience strategy should be smooth and easy to access, with all the platforms working holistically together to provide the best customer experience. It should be an approach that allows customers to move between channels seamlessly without losing context.

Maintaining Online Ethics

Wanting to get yourself noticed means daring to be different through continued reinvention and a willingness to embrace new things, which was discussed in Chapter 15, "Step 6: Do You Need a Brand Makeover?" This is an important part of building a lasting social media success story, but remember to keep your ethics in tact along the way.

A good example of this is in the use of Twitter *hashtags*, defined by Twitter as being "used to mark keywords or topics in a tweet and created organically by Twitter users as a way to categorize messages." For example, tweets about the 2010 World Cup had the hashtag #WorldCup, meaning that whenever people searched for this topic, tweets with the hashtag appeared. Hashtags are a great way to follow issues of interest and are used extensively to denote news events around the world.

Remember that customers like to jump between platforms when searching for information or trying to resolve an issue.

Habitat, a leading British furniture retailer, with more than 80 stores across Europe, decided to jump aboard the social media bandwagon by starting a Twitter page and got off on the right track with a pleasant Twitter presence that reflected the company's clean branding. However, their lack of social media ethics soon landed them in hot water.

To generate traffic to their Twitter outpost, Habitat used various hashtags in their tweets to appear in popular topics of discussion, but they chose to use hashtags that were completely irrelevant to the content of their tweets and had nothing to do with furniture, shopping, or renovating. Instead, they made the mistake of merely putting in popular hashtags at the time of their post. They used hashtags such as #iPhone, #Apple, and even ones relating to tweets about the war in #Iraq. Clearly, Habitat saw this as an opportunity to generate greater brand awareness because by using these hashtags they would appear in the most popular searches. The result for end users was that when they searched (for example, #iPhone), Habitat's tweet would appear, but users found it had nothing to do with their search. Obviously, Twitter users viewed this very negatively and heavily criticized the upscale furniture company for piggybacking the popular topics to send spam.

In response to the backlash, Habitat deleted their spamming tweets. Unfortunately for them, however, they remained viewable via Twitter search, which has done nothing to help their brand image. Clearly, Habitat opted to put consideration for their customers' online needs and their ethics aside in a bid to drive traffic to them. They didn't strategize about how to bring value or generate conversations about their brand. Instead, they created spam by piggybacking on popular topics. Since then, Habitat has apologized[2] and has been working to make amends for its lapse in ethical social media use, but the damage caused could well have been socially lethal for its brand image.

---

2. Habitat blames intern for Twitter PR Disaster: http://news.sky.com/home/business/article/15319105

Utilizing Social Media Metrics

Understanding how social media is being used by your audience and how your particular platforms are being accessed, and from where, is vital to evolving your social media strategy in a way that will bring you the biggest *Return on Investment* (ROI).

We cover this very important area more comprehensively in Chapter 19, "Step 10: Knowing You've Made It and Measuring Your Success," but for now let's look at some of the basics that are essential for you to understand and employ if you are to become one of the social media fittest.

When thinking about your social media strategy, you should be planning for six important metric areas. These can be viewed as three different levels of social media participation multiplied by two different types of determining metrics, namely qualitative and quantitative analysis, and are broken down as follows:

- **Activity:** Any metrics relating to actions your organization is taking in social media: blogging, tweeting, posting, promoting, and so on.

- **Interaction:** This category's metrics focus on how your audience is engaging with your social media presence: followers, comments, likes, sharing, user-created content, and so on.

- **Returns:** This group measures your social media activities driving revenue creation (and the activities that lead up to it), cost minimization (along with activities to help achieve it), and other critical financial performance metrics.

In the next chapter we show you how to use a metrics strategy for these elements that will provide you with the most complete evaluative picture of your social media strategy.

It is vital to continue to adapt and evolve our approach to social media by finding new ways to integrate it into the customer experience.

Adapting and Evolving

To become one of the social media fittest, it is vital to continue to adapt and evolve your approach to its use by finding new ways to integrate the customer experience. A good example of this is the company Best Buy, which initiated an experiment with Shopkick, a company that delivers location-based shopping experiences at retail stores through a consumer's smartphone.

Rather than hide from in-store comparison shopping on mobile devices, this app enables consumers to earn and redeem kickbucks when they use it inside of a Best Buy store to access information about products, tell friends about products, or make purchases. Best Buy reinforced the use of shopkick through their website, blogs, and tweets, evolving the concept from a store-centered to a total social media-centric one.

Another innovative use of social media came from Ford, who broke with traditional television-centric forms of media plans to invest in digital advertising. Before the launch of their new Ford Fiesta, they created viral buzz about the car through a network of 100 bloggers who tested and wrote about it for their readers. In 2010, Ford launched the Fiesta Project on YouTube (youtube.com/user/FordFiesta) to capture user-generated video about their new car (see Figure 18-1). It was a huge success and has marked the way forward for future car launches, saving them 90% on their previous promotional launch budgets in the process.

(Source: Youtube.com/user/FordFiesta).

Figure 18-1   The Fiesta Project implemented by Ford showed great creativity in their use of social media and saved them 90% on previous new car launch spends.

The trick we can learn from these examples is to keep thinking of new and exciting ways to keep our audience informed and entertained. Do this, and your business will be well on its way to not only surviving but also thriving in the world of social media.

19

Step 10: Knowing You've Made It and Measuring Your Success

You've already come such a long way on your social media journey and have hopefully now begun to embrace the beneficial effects it has had (and will continue to have) on your brand. However, as with all long-distance travel, there comes a point when you need to stop for a spell and assess just how far you have journeyed toward your intended destination (in this case, that of social media success).

But just how do we define *success* in social media terms? The obvious point of reference is the number of followers, subscribers, friends, and connections you have accumulated along your way, yes? Well, yes and no actually. Building your network is, of course, vital to being taken seriously and becoming a key influencer, but always remember that it's quality over quantity that truly matters. So we can consider the ultimate social media success to be measured in terms of the perfect blend, that of quality *and* quantity combined into a powerhouse network that can be engaged with daily to grow and grow your business and brand.

So now it's time to take a closer look at what you've learned and what you've gained from a wider perspective to fully appreciate just how much clout your social media presence has managed to achieve to date.

The basic metrics of number of visits to your blog (or website) coupled with what platforms are driving them there are always a good starting point for this exercise, particularly when tracked alongside your social media network of fans, friends, and followers. Another key metric to plot regularly is that of mentions, discussions, or comments on your brand or product. These are all great ways of providing you with a wide view of how your social media efforts are fairing but will fall short of both giving you the information you truly need to build an in-depth analysis of your online star status and of providing you with the necessary tools to improve upon it.

How to Get a High-Definition Picture of Your Success to Date

To see the big picture in high definition, you need a formula that provides greater clarity to the work you have put into social media so far, shows whether you have strayed from your intended path, and if so, arms you with the knowledge to quickly find your route back to it again.

The following sections draw from everything you have learned within this book so far and condense these key lessons into a checklist for effective success measurement.

Find Your Elite Social Drivers

Discover the most valuable traffic-driving sources across your social media platforms and rate each one to provide a top-down list of what and who's working the hardest on your brand's behalf. You'll find some key drivers that are, in essence, your A-listers or elite driving forces for your social media brand presence. Use tools such as Sprout Social (home.sproutsocial.com/social-monitoring) to track them and provide all the necessary stats you need, and others such as Klout (klout.com) and PeerIndex (peerindex.com) to keep tabs on those you influence the most and, likewise, those you are most influenced by.

Track Audience Duration and Discover Their Preferences

Instead of focusing solely on the number of blog page views, look at how much time your social network audience spends viewing your content or using your online applications. Pay particular attention to whether the usage per visitor is increasing or decreasing over time and look at the posts that achieve the longest audience duration periods. For example, if your blog is getting a lot of hits, but people are leaving quickly, there's a strong possibility that you're making mistakes in your layout or content. Whether it's trouble finding the information they're looking for, or that the content you're providing simply isn't stimulating enough, duration monitoring is the best way to ensure you keep on top of what your social media audience require to keep them coming back for more. A number of great free and low-cost tools are available to measure duration and other valuable visitor data, including W3Counter (w3counter.com), OpenTracker (Opentracker.net), and Footprint (footprintlive.com/live).

When our @grattongirl and @grattonboy brands started to really take off on the social media circuit, we found this kind of measurement particularly valuable because it enabled us to target different types of content to certain social media tribes within our overall audience based on categories of interest and media delivery preferences, as illustrated in Figure 19-1 and Figure 19-2. Some absolutely love reading our marketing and technology articles, for example, and spend a considerable amount of time studying, absorbing, and commenting on them. Others prefer the immediacy of our videoclips, infographics, and images. When you take the time to study duration preferences among your audience, you empower yourself with the ability to group them in a way that allows for valuable, targeted content to be provided to them on a daily basis.

Figure 19-1   @grattongirl's audience can be divided into segments based on interest, which can be used to tailor content.

Figure 19-2 @grattonboy's audience can similarly be divided into segments for ease of content planning.

Track Your Audience Growth

Consider the pattern of growth you are experiencing across your social media platforms and chart this in terms of numbers over time to show a percentage of growth that will enable you to review consistency in effort and reward in terms of growth for time spent. As a rule of thumb, a good steady social media growth pattern suggests that you are providing your audience with consistently valuable content, but there are lessons to be learned from monitoring the peaks and troughs of growth too. For example, a sudden slowing of Twitter following growth might be due to nothing more than a season change, where people are tending to travel on vacation and might not have access to the Internet or during holiday periods such as Christmas and the New Year, when time spent with family generally takes precedence over the time spent online.

Monitor Your Audience Activity Ratio

Keep a record of the comparison between the number of currently active members alongside the overall total number of members and chart this ratio over time. Remember that you'll, without a doubt, always have some inactive members. Keep an eye on these and use tools such as Tweepi (Tweepi.com) to monitor inactivity for excessive periods of time and to flush those users from your network. In terms of your efforts to increase interaction with your audience, this metric can prove particularly valuable in measuring how effective they have been.

Google Analytics *Custom Segments* provide an effective and relatively easy-to-use way of tracking visitors from social media channels. First, sign up to Google Analytics (google.com/analytics), click **Open the advanced segments**, and select **Create a new advanced segment**, as shown in Figure 19-3.

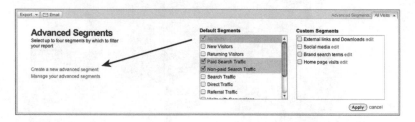

(Source: Google.com)

Figure 19-3   Google Analytics Advanced Segments are a valuable and fairly easy-to-use tool.

This will take you to another screen from where you can select the various parameters for your segment, see Figure 19-4. You can select the social media channels for your segment as follows:

1. Open the **Traffic Sources** from the Dimensions section.

2. Drag the **Source** to your segment area.

3. Set the Condition to **Contains**.

4. In the Value field, identify which of your social channels you wish to track using the segment. You can also use value fields in advanced segments to monitor particular areas of interest from followers and visitors.

5. Click **Add** or **Statement**, as needed.

6. Name the segment and click **Test Segment** to verify that everything is working. Doing so shows you how many visits each part of the segment contains.

If you have more than one Google Analytics account, you can select where the segment is available from in the drop-down list. Now you can click **Save** and **Apply to Report**, and you will see the statistics for only this segment. When you want to apply the segment to your statistics, you can select it from any page within Google Analytics by selecting it from the available drop-down menu. Comparing visitor numbers is a great indication as to whether your efforts are bearing fruit.

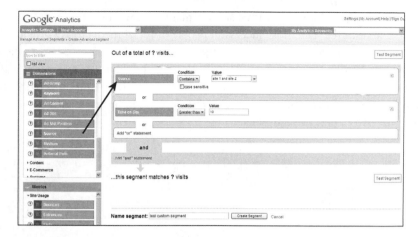

(Source: Google.com)

Figure 19-4   Setting the various parameters within Advanced Segments.

Don't Forget Your Share of Voice

We've already covered how to understand and work with your *Share of Voice* (SoV) back in Chapter 11, "Step 2: Understand and Build Your Social Media Voice," and now you're going to use it to the full as part of your success measurement toolkit. It ties in well with the preceding segment on audience activity because it considers how often your company and its products are mentioned on the social Web. To add a reference point to your social-mention tracking, create an SoV report based on the number of times your company, brand, and products are mentioned over a 30-day period in a negative, neutral, or positive context in relation to your competitors. You'll need to use a social media listening tool for this, such as Social Mention (socialmention.com), Radian6 (radian6.com), or any of the many others available online to establish how often you, versus your competitors, are mentioned (neutral or positive) during the same 30 days.

Add up all mentions for the category (you plus your competitors) and then divide your mentions by the total to calculate your SoV—which is always a percentage. If you've forgotten how all this works, you might want to take a quick trip back to Chapter 11 to refresh your memory.

And We Made It

So there you have it! Your 10-step plan to social media superstardom for your business and brand. If you've reached your target goals by the time you get to this point of the book, congratulations. If not, keep going with your final destination firmly in mind and remember that the plan is always here to refer to if you need reassurance along the way.

To round things off, we have a final section that we know you'll find to be an invaluable resource. The most successful people in social media today provide their unique and exclusive insights into success that you can draw upon 24/7 or whenever you feel a need for their incredible inspiration and advice. We came up with various titles for the section, but in the end there was only one that was truly applicable because it sums up exactly what this book offers in terms of social media guidance: "An Expert in Your Pocket."

An Expert in Your Pocket

20

Jeff Bullas

"The power of social media to spread your brand, influence an audience, and be ubiquitous continues to surprise me."
—Jeff Bullas

About Jeff Bullas

Jeff Bullas is a social media speaker, blogger, and strategist and works with companies and executives to optimize their online personal and company presence and brands through social media channels and other web technologies.

Jeff has a degree in commerce and economics and has spent most of his career involved with information technologies, telecommunications, and the Web.

His blog (JeffBullas.com) is subscribed to by more than 120,000 readers. It focuses on social media and digital marketing, including how to use Twitter, blogging, Facebook, YouTube, LinkedIn, and *search engine optimization* (SEO) to assist businesses in "getting found online" in an increasingly digital world. Jeff's blog is currently rated as one of the top 100 global marketing blogs by Adage.com.

Expert Answers to Key Social Media Questions

How Has Social Media Benefited Your Business/Personal Brand?

The reality is that social media has given me a global audience that I could not have hoped to achieve through traditional means. I have been invited to speak all around the world and have been approached by a major publisher to write a book. It has put me in contact with senior executives at major brands, including Ford, General Motors, and the world's largest advertising agency.

The power of social media to spread your brand, influence an audience, and be ubiquitous continues to surprise me.

How and Why Do You Use Twitter?

Twitter is a tool that I use as a platform to market my blog. The reasons I use it include the following:

- You can create a following on Twitter that is specific to your target markets and audience. This is a secret that most people don't understand.

- It is instant; as soon as I have published my latest blog I can spread it to other influential Twitter "friends" as well as tweet it myself.

> Social media is about the personal and social aspect of the Web that previously didn't exist.

What Tips Do You Have Concerning Twitter Names (or Handles) and Avatars?

Social media is about the personal and social aspect of the Web that didn't exist for the first decade after the Web became publicly visible with the invention of the browser.

So if you are a personal brand, use your own photo and real name, as this is consistent with the social Web that is now pervasive. However, if you are a business brand, maintaining the branding consistency and publishing your brand's logo on Twitter is the accepted norm.

How and Why Do You Use Facebook?

I use Facebook both personally and as a "page" for Jeffbullas.com as the Facebook presence for my blog.

Facebook has almost become the social media channel of choice for most of the developed world, and like Twitter, it is a platform you cannot ignore if you want your ideas and content to spread.

So why do I use Facebook? I use it to publish my blog posts and interact with my readers because it is where they are hanging out.

How and Why Do You Use YouTube?

YouTube is very important for two reasons:

- It is the second largest search engine after Google.

- You have a 53 times better chance than Google for appearing at the top of search results according to Forrester Research.

Creating great video content is about being authentic, and I use a Flipcam to interview other people and put out short tips on how to use social media for business.

Facebook has become the social media channel of choice for most of the developed world and is a platform you cannot ignore if you want your ideas and content to spread.

You can take it with you to conferences and conduct spontaneous interviews. Just like a blog, it can educate and entertain while you sleep. Traditional media, such as television, is a one-time show, whereas YouTube has longevity that provides enduring content.

How and Why Do You Use LinkedIn?

LinkedIn is a great place to network with other executives and with a user base of more than 100 million is a major social network that provides a channel to connect and engage with other influencers.

The three major ways I use LinkedIn are as follows:

- To publish my blog posts. (There is an app on LinkedIn that enables you to publish your WordPress blog to your profile.)

- To network with other executives and influencers.

- To position myself as an expert and authority in my industry by participating in Groups on LinkedIn and the Q&A platform within the LinkedIn platform.

What Advice Can You Give to Newbie Bloggers?

- Buy your own domain with your own name. (It doesn't have to be a dot com; if it isn't available, use another domain suffix, such as dot biz.) If you don't want to use your own name, obtain a domain name that gives you a notable brand presence within your industry.

- Purchase a blogging template (if financial resources allow), such as a WordPress Thesis theme. This is flexible and great for SEO (and usually can be bought for less than $100).

- I prefer my blog to be self-hosted, not hosted free with services such as WordPress or TypePad. I believe this creates much more flexibility in the future to improve your blog through widgets that aren't possible within a third-party blogging environment.

- Have the blog professionally designed and developed if you have the financial resources to do so.

- Write posts regularly, at least once a week (more if you can, with two or three times better, but at least once a day is best).

- Publish any content online you have offline.

- Use great headlines. This is the bait to get someone to read further.

- Write comments on other important bloggers posts in your industry.

- Place your blog content on other social media sites, such as Facebook, YouTube, LinkedIn, and Twitter, to leverage your content.

- Use bullet points to make it easy for readers to scan your blog posts to obtain the important points.

- Add credibility banners such as how many subscribers, number of hits, blog grade, and any awards as your blog gains traction.

- Provide "share this" buttons to Facebook and Twitter, as a minimum.

- From day one, implement the feature to sub-scribe to your blog either with RSS or email. Google's FeedBurner makes this easy to implement.

- Use images to add some style to the blog. These can be easily copied into your blog using free images from Flickr's advanced search creative commons license.

- Promote your blog on Twitter.

In my experience, major components to make a blog successful include the following:

- The Twitter retweet button (makes it easy for people to share your content).

- The Facebook share button (again, makes it easy to share).

- Credibilty banners, such as the number of Twitter followers and awards won, can go a long way to displaying and quantifying credibility.

- Facebook social plug-ins, so people can "like" your Facebook page when visiting your blog.

Self-hosting your blog creates far more flexibility to improve your blog through the addition of widgets that aren't possible within a third-party environment.

- A subscribe by email feature.

- Buttons that allow people to subscribe to your social media channels.

How Much Time Do You Spend Each Day on Social Media Activities?

I spend two to three hours researching and writing my blog post five days a week. I also spend approximately 15 to 30 minutes marketing the post on the major social networking platforms.

> If you're not passionate about your topic, don't start blogging about it.

I have two time-management tips here:

- Turn Twitter off so that you are not distracted while performing focused writing.

- Rise early so that you can have quiet dedicated time to write your blog. (I get up at 4.30 a.m., five days a week.)

So a dedicated time without distractions and discipline are essential to making a blogger successful. This is made easier if you are passionate about what you do.

Jeff's Top Tips for Social Media Success

- If you're not passionate about your topic, don't start blogging about it.

- Know who your target audience is.

- Write or publish text or video content for your audience that is topical, answers problems, and provide how-to advice.

- Connect with other social media influencers in your industry.

- Share their content.

- Read, read, read, and then read even more about your topics. (Mine are Facebook, Twitter, YouTube, and LinkedIn.)

- Don't be afraid to fail *small* and fail *often*. Waiting to publish while making it perfect means it will never happen. Just "ship it!"

21

Lori McNee

"The very fact that I am included in this book is a true testament to the marketing power of social media."
—Lori McNee

About Lori McNee

For more than 25 years, Lori McNee has lived with her family in the beautiful Rocky Mountains of central Idaho. A native of California and raised in the Southwest, Lori cultivated her interest in art and wildlife during her childhood. Today, Lori is an internationally recognized professional artist and art-marketing expert whose broad spectrum of artwork includes still life, landscape, and nature paintings.

Along with her fine arts business, Lori also juggles a professional blogging, writing, and public-speaking career. She freely shares valuable fine arts tips and art business and social media advice on her popular blog FineArtTips.com. Lori ranks as one of the "Most Influential Artists" on Twitter and "The Top 100 Most Powerful Women on Twitter." Lori is also a television hostess for Plum TV and has been featured in magazines, books, and blogs, including, *The Huffington Post, Los Angeles Times, North Light Book's Artist's & Graphic Designer's Market, Photographer's Market, Southwest Art Magazine, Wildscapes Magazine, American Art Collector, Money Dummy Blog, Artists Network, Art Bistro,* and *Art Talk Magazine* (to name a few). Lori has also been named among the "Top 10 Up and Coming Women Bloggers" and as one of "Twitter's Top 75 Badass Women." In addition, Lori is on the board of advisors for *Plein Air Magazine*.

Lori is a member of Oil Painters of America. Her sought-after original oil paintings are sold in galleries throughout the United States and on her blog, LoriMcNee.com.

Expert Answers to Key Social Media Questions

How Has Social Media Benefited Your Business/Personal Brand?

When I embarked upon my social media journey back in 2009, I had no idea how it would affect the course of my fine arts career. During this time, as with most small businesses, the art industry was feeling the pinch of a struggling global economy. Instead of taking a passive approach, I hit the force head on, started two blogs, and began using social media as a way to strengthen my art business and personal brand. It's a way of obtaining large-scale reach for little or no cost other than my time, and it eliminates the middleman, providing me with the unique opportunity to have a direct relationship with my customers.

In less than two years, my personal brand has grown and is now internationally known. My art career is flourishing when others in my industry are laboring. Meanwhile, the FineArtTips.com and LoriMcNee.com blogs are growing, and my paintings are consistently being featured in national and international magazines. I am now writing for books, blogging for the art industry's leading blogs, working as a television hostess, and garnering recognition by world-renowned media giants, including *The Huffington Post*—all because of social media.

How and Why Do You Use Twitter?

Twitter has been the lifeblood to my blogs and art business. It's possibly the most intimidating social platform because everything happens so quickly, but once you jump in and start engaging, you will see that it also has the broadest reach. I use Twitter to post informative links and drive large amounts of traffic back to my blogs. I find it to be the fastest way to build brand recognition for my art business.

When I first started Twitter back in 2009, my target niche was primarily artists and art collectors. To my surprise, my tweets and blog posts began to capture the attention of a much broader audience.

Why? My Twitter updates have an appeal that *reaches beyond my own art niche.* How? I am able to reach beyond my art readers by understanding that most people have broad interests. I tweet about art, and share my other interests, which include blogging, social media, nature, quotes, photography, outdoors, and more.

Not only can I attract my own niche readers, I can also appeal to multiple audience profiles while staying true to my target audience. Stray from your own niche to apply this approach to your own social media strategy.

The key to my Twitter success is that I actively engage with my followers and do not focus on selling but rather on giving.

The key to my Twitter success is that I actively engage with my followers and do not focus on selling but rather on giving. I have learned to speak with my audience, not at them. By engaging with my market, I am creating a community around my brand, and this leads to trust and sales.

Twitter is much like a cocktail party where you can quickly meet and exchange information. But the social etiquette rules still apply. Would you just walk up to an acquaintance and say, "Hey, please buy my product." No, that is just rude. You need to connect and build a relationship first.

Remember, Twitter is microblogging, and your followers are looking for tweets with value. About 80% of my tweets and retweets share useful information and resources, including links to my blogs or other social media channels. The remaining 20% of the tweets are spent genuinely reaching out to my following with small talk, inquiries, and relationship building.

What Tips Do You Have Concerning Twitter Names (or Handles) and Avatars?

Your name is the first thing that people will see on Twitter. Use the name you want to represent your brand. For example, I am an artist, and my name is my brand.

When I first started on Twitter, I used @lorimcnee as my ID. However, I quickly changed my Twitter handle to @lorimcneeartist and rapidly gained loyal followers.

Why? Because it is easier for people to instantly associate me as an artist this way. Also when people do a Twitter search for *artist*, my name appears. This is a tactic to consider.

It has been my personal experience that it is best for small businesses and solopreneurs to use their real names along with an image of themselves, rather than an impersonal company name and logo.

It is also important to use a friendly profile picture. Your avatar affects how a message is received and also how individuals interpret it, so make sure yours is warm and inviting.

To further your brand identity, it is a good idea to use the same avatar on all of your social media sites. Go ahead and change your photo, but be forewarned this may confuse some of your followers. It is best to wait until you have a loyal following before you make these kinds of changes.

How and Why Do You Use Facebook?

Honestly, when I first started Facebook I thought it was primarily to keep in touch with family and friends. But I have come to understand Facebook to be an invaluable marketing tool that works hand-in-hand with Twitter.

Having said that, Facebook is entirely different as a platform. If Twitter is a cocktail party, then Facebook is more like a *dinner party* where you build on conversations and further develop your relationships.

Facebook is an ideal platform for the social butterfly, and I use it to connect with people and prospective customers whom I have already met and who share similar interests. It's also a great way of keeping in touch with family and friends. In fact, Facebook has replaced email, chat, and photo sharing for many users.

> If Twitter is a cocktail party, then Facebook is more like a dinner party.

I find that both a Facebook profile and the fan page are useful for my business. I use my profile to network and promote my personal brand while using my fan page to promote my art business.

How and Why Do You Use YouTube?

YouTube is a fun and creative way for me to broaden my brand. I consider video marketing an integral component of my social media strategy. With this in mind, I find it's important to gear videos toward your audience, such as how-to demonstrations, product reviews, interviews, and special announcements applicable to your product, service, or brand.

The most popular videos average around three minutes in length, so I find it's best to keep mine short and meaningful.

I use my other social media networks like Twitter and Facebook to virally market my videos.

What Advice Can You Give to Newbie Bloggers?

A blog is the easiest way for potential customers to discover your business or brand.

A blog is the easiest way for potential customers to discover your business or brand and its associated website. Nowadays, blogging is fast becoming an integral component to any small to midsize business plan.

It's is a must to keep your content current and to fully utilize the available technologies within your blog. For example, you can easily embed video, audio podcasts, or images into your posts. Also be sure to integrate widgets for your social media platforms (including Facebook Like buttons, Tweet This, and Share, for example) to drive traffic to your social media networks and make it easy for your readers to distribute your interesting content.

Make your blog visually appealing and easy to navigate and remember *content is king*. Find your own voice and write about things that nobody else writes about. Offer services and sell your brand by adding value.

Lori's Top Tips for Social Media Success

- Be a good Twitter follower. Do not forget the "little guy" as your following grows. Remember your followers have helped you get to where you are now and that they are loyal. Reach out to them and show your appreciation.

- Social media is *a dialog*, not *a monolog*! Be authentic and engage.

- Make sure your last tweet counts. At the end of each Twitter session, leave a valuable tweet. Your potential followers will judge whether or not to follow you by your last Twitter update.

- Realize this: *Compensation comes in many forms*. Yes, I have sold artwork via Twitter and Facebook, but more important, social media has provided me with unique business opportunities and relationships that would never have happened without this new marketing medium.

- It is imperative to remember that social media is about giving. It is about *we*, not about *me*. You cannot expect to receive with a closed fist, and so *tweet others the way you would like to be tweeted*. When you understand this, you will recognize how to use social media as a powerful marketing medium for your business.

22

Paul Steele

"Being social on social media has enabled me to help many others achieve their goals."
—Paul Steele

About Paul Steele

Paul Steele is one of the most popular travel bloggers on Twitter, has been mentioned in the national press, and has regular travel articles in *The Huffington Post*.

In Paul's own words, "Having spent 16 years slightly cocooned in an army career and all the traveling and turmoil that occurs with that, I can look back and also say the experiences gained along the way have brought me to a great point. I like to think glass half full in all I do and goals/challenges are there to help me forward not stop me.

Since leaving in 2005, I have gone from a daily grind of sitting behind a desk eight hours a day punching numbers into a PC to being able to appreciate all life throws at me and getting out and away as much as possible.

Hiking and trekking are my main pursuits. Inactivity for three years behind the desk gained me a few pounds around the waist, and one day I was looking at a picture of Kilimanjaro in a magazine and thought, why not? So off I went, loved the experience, and went on to more. Mt. Aconcagua, Argentina, long-distance treks in a whole plethora of extremes, and all this increases my hunger for more (including an upcoming South Pole trek), more often than not helping great charities too.

One thing I have valued from all this is seeing others inspired to follow on and enjoy something they thought they never could. The tweetup and hikes/climbs have allowed me to share my experiences in person, not just in 140 characters or in pictures. There are so many people out there who have looked at, say, a U.K. mountain and only thought in their heads that they wish to be up there. I have helped many to achieve these goals. Being social on social media is one big and main thing that has enabled this. Being open and respectful answering questions and being positive without fakeness helps people feel they want to join in.

Obviously, as you travel you experience more and more. This creates more hunger, and thus the cycle goes on. I appreciate, enjoy the moments, cherish the friendships, and am open to all ideas. Who knows what is next?"

Expert Answers to Key Social Media Questions

How Has Social Media Benefited Your Business/Personal Brand?

Social media helps to show what people are up to within the parameters of what they allow or want. There is no wrong or right, but there are personal preferences, and I respect all.

What has helped me personally is the fact I have never auto-tweeted and have kept variety. This combined with sharing and seeking others with their own passions has been something I think works for me, alongside keeping positive and never showing negativity online toward others. After all, who are we to judge someone harshly from behind 140 characters?

How and Why Do You Use Twitter?

Great question! Why? I started on Twitter when a friend introduced me to it. No business, no agenda, no barriers. I avoided niches and thus learned lots from all corners of the world. I tweet a lot, and for me, 90% of this is done from my iPhone. This has helped me to maintain my outdoor activities while being there on Twitter and seeing/sharing what others are doing as well as what I am up to "on the go."

> I tweet a lot, and for me, 90% of this is done from my iPhone.

What Tips Do You Have Concerning Twitter Names (or Handles) and Avatars?

When I joined Twitter, I was just me. No brand, no company, no blog. So my username was me, plain and simple. What this does is makes me look more personable, I guess. You see comments and advice on this all over the blogosphere. Again, it is personal choice, but I think people are more likely to trust a real name and real picture rather than an obscure name and branded or unbranded random picture.

How and Why Do You Use Facebook?

Ah, Facebook. I use it, but on a more catching-up/keeping-up basis. I have lots of old friends on there as well as new. The pace is much slower there, and I have resisted the temptation to use it à la Twitter. Facebook friends would not appreciate an update every minute as in a twitterfeed. I am thus a more casual user, dropping in every day or two to see what people are up to or to catch up with an old friend in more than 140 characters.

> The pace is much slower on Facebook, and I have resisted the temptation to use it à la Twitter.

How and Why Do You Use YouTube?

YouTube itself as a social tool has lost its way for me a little. True, it's a great tool for uploading your videos and for embedding them onto sites, but I find it a shame that visitors to the site inevitably get drawn toward YouTube's newfound commercialism. Twitter and Facebook are better platforms for me to see and share what is on there socially via the embedding of YouTube content.

How and Why Do You Use LinkedIn?

I have a LinkedIn account and use it. If someone seems interesting to you, LinkedIn provides a great way to find a fully expanded personal profile in great form, curriculum vitae/resumé and all. Twitter/Facebook profiles are restrictive in characters/subjects, so LinkedIn enables people to open up their business profiles.

What Advice Can You Give to Newbie Bloggers?

My blog baldhiker.com came more as a labor of love. I had been on Twitter for more than two years before I even started it. People were constantly asking questions about my TwitPics and hiking tweets, and I thought I should have a platform to expand my thoughts and experiences in travel, mountains, and learning.

My advice to newbies? Enjoy it, write personably, write what you feel without trying too hard, and you will get into comfortable zones/niches. Never worry about readership or targets on a blog. I feel that this creates falseness and disconnection. All will come in time. Think whose blogs you enjoy and use them as mentors to help you find your individual style.

I think the most successful blogs have a personal touch with a human behind them. Visuals are great, too, as they provide clarity and enhancement to the content.

How Much Time Do You Spend Each Day on Social Media Activities?

Time on social media? Ha ha, it seems all day. Yes, as I said before, I use my iPhone for tweeting and keeping up with my social media friends, no matter where I am or what I am doing. Lots of people know that when I am tweeting away about normal things I could actually be standing on a mountain or hill at the time. I never auto-tweet. If I'm busy, I'm busy; if I'm tweeting, I'm there. Why should I expect people to be sociable with me if I am not there and just on a feed?

Real friends will understand if you are busy.

> The most successful blogs are those that have a personal touch with a "human" behind them.

Paul's Top Tips for Social Media Success

- Be real.
- Be positive.
- Be sincere.
- Help others.
- Share with others.
- Learn from others.
- Be open minded.
- Never think negatively about others you hardly know.
- If you are all about "me, me, me," you can't expect people to respect or follow you.

23

Jessica Northey

"If you are not utilizing social media to its full extent, you are missing the opportunity to grow your own voice."

—Jessica Northey

About Jessica Northey

Tucson native Jessica Northey is taking over country music and radio one tweet at a time, specializing in using social media to break new artists. And within broadcasting, her optimization techniques are being implemented at top stations across the United States.

A writer, blogger, nationally recognized speaker, on-air personality, and social PR expert who owns social media boutique firm Finger Candy Media, LLC, Jessica has a personal network of more than 170,000 followers and is consistently ranked in the top 500 most influential people on Twitter.

With over 15 years of media experience, including television and radio, Jessica is the associate editor and social media expert for FullThrottleCountry.com, country music radio's interactive idea-sharing new media platform. According to their managing editor, Chuck Geiger, "Jessica *is* social media." She is also co-founder/contributor of KrisCountry.com and country music news aggregate Twitter.com/ KrisCountry and is a contributor to the Nashville Music Guide. Jessica is a highly regarded speaker and has presented at Radio's Conclave and at the Walter Cronkite School of Journalism 140 Character Twitter Conference.

Expert Answers to Key Social Media Questions

How Has Social Media Benefited Your Business/Personal Brand?

Social media is perfect for anyone who wants to control their brand's message or create a network of support and be heard by thousands of targeted individuals, with the potential to reach millions. If you are not utilizing social media to its full extent, you are missing the opportunity to grow your own voice.

Social media and social networking are the fundamental building blocks of my personal brand and my company Finger Candy Media, LLC. I use social media as though it were my own broadcasting station and through consistent social networking, including blogging, Twitter, Facebook, and LinkedIn utilization.

How and Why Do You Use Twitter?

I use Twitter for fun and to discover new and interesting people, places, and things. Strategically, I align myself with people in my industry or stations that are playing my clients' music.

Nowadays, I follow a lot of entertainment industry folks. I used to follow a lot of social media people but then realized they don't pay my bills and in some ways are my competition.

When it comes to following back, I don't have a lot of rules of engagement. I honestly follow people I think are interesting and that I am genuinely interested in.

Do You Think Using Your Real Name (or Surname) in Your Twitter ID (or Any Other Profile ID) Is Good or Is Using Your Company/Brand Name Better?

I come from a traditional media background where most people use a "stage name," but I personally feel that my many years in broadcasting have helped me build and brand my own name, which I continue to use.

What Tips Do You Have Concerning Providing Good Social Media Content?

> I align myself on Twitter with people in my industry or stations that are playing my clients' music.

When it comes to content, I look for interesting articles, blog posts, photos, videos, and people and share these findings with my audience. The information I look for and distribute is a direct relation to the things that interest me and in turn that seem to interest many of my followers, based on the number of retweets I get.

I take my role as a person who cares what I pass on to people very seriously. I wouldn't share something with my audience that I didn't personally find fascinating.

When it comes to news, I use twitterfeeds to direct real-time news from trusted sources to my Twitter stream. I say *trusted* because I have worked in and around news and news delivery for a long time and get my raw data news from the *Associated Press* (AP). I also get content/news from AllAccess, Full Throttle Country, KrisCountry, Chris Brogan's website, and a few other industry-related blog feeds.

> I wouldn't share something with my audience that I didn't personally find fascinating.

How and Why Do You Use Facebook?

I use Facebook in a more personal way than other social media platforms. I keep it close to my chest and tend to connect primarily with real-life friends, family, and clients.

How and Why Do You Use YouTube and What Advice Would You Give to Anyone Wishing to Put Together a YouTube Video?

I don't make a lot of videos, but my clients do. Here are a few tips for attempting to make a viral video that I pass along to them:

- The more homemade your video looks, the better it works.

- Your videos should only be 30 seconds to three minutes max.

- Be very clear and specific about what you are doing.

- Where possible, your video should be entertaining. Funny stuff seems to spread the quickest.

- Make it look as spontaneous as possible.

- Tell everyone about it.

- Get it out to friends with lots of followers.

- If you don't succeed, just keep trying.

> The potential of online video is obvious; it could be your next big ticket!

I am still making my way into using online video. It's become a part of how I get information, and I am trying to integrate video into my personal marketing strategy. The potential of online video is obvious: It could be your big ticket.

What Advice Can You Give to Newbie Bloggers?

If you're serious about sharing your ideas and beliefs and building a stronger relationship with others, you need to add full-on blogging to your marketing tools. You can also use blogging to provide more content to your Twitter and Facebook accounts.

Here are the reasons why I think everyone should be blogging consistently:

- Blogging shows what you are about, along with your passion and ideas about what you do.

- You can bounce ideas off others and get feedback about projects you are working on.

- You provide content to the rest of the Web. I have my blog picked up by news feeds all the time, and I use other people's blogs to get my point across.

- You can get great analytics from your blog to see what sites are feeding it.

- If you have varied interests, you can bring them all together in your blog.

How Much Time Do You Spend on Social Media Activities Each Day and How Important Do You Think Social Media Time Management Is?

> I have my blog picked up by news feeds all the time, and I use other people's blogs to get my point across.

Every week it varies, but I am a workaholic. I have more than 30 clients, so my day is divided among all of them. I generally spend 33% of my working day on my personal content, 33% on maintenance for clients, and 33% on monitoring others.

Jessica's Top Tips for Social Media Success

- Have a direction and start with a clear statement of goals. For example, are you looking to connect with others or drive traffic to a website? Determine your key metrics *before* you get started and pick three solid metrics to track (for example, Web/blog traffic, number of targeted followers in a certain time, sales conversions).

- Before you begin, worry about social media tools last, not first. Tools will change. (Remember AOL, Yahoo!, MySpace?) If you have a solid strategy for who you are trying to reach, it will translate across all platforms.

- Understand how your target audience uses social media (by gender, age, geography, and so on). Are they on Facebook, Twitter, Foursquare, blogging, YouTube, LinkedIn? You need to be where they are.

- Create an interesting bio. This is your headline and might be your only chance to catch someone's attention. Include your website/blog URL.

- Use a great photo if possible, but if you have to use a logo, make sure it is clear and gets your brand message across effectively.

- Use the background space on your Twitter profile to incorporate your logo or things you are interested in.

- Remember that content is king, but consistency is his queen.

- Devote time to social media housekeeping and maintenance. If you want results, start with 30 minutes a day. Post in the morning and then check in the evening. These are also the highest-usage times of the day, early morning and early evening.

- Promote Twitter on Facebook, Facebook on your blog, YouTube on Twitter, and so on. Add social media platform participation links to your business card, letterhead, vehicle wrap, broadcast, and print media. Consistently talk about it when you are out in public. You can even add social media applications to your cell phone. Try running social media-only promotional offers and put a deadline in place to track the sales.

- A social media plan should mirror your marketing plan, complement your traditional media goals, and engage consumers while providing meaningful, relevant, and personalized content direct to your consumer. Once you have identified your purpose, you will have a clear strategy direction for social media optimization. Try not to overthink, but do act with purpose.

24

Danny Devriendt

"Like fine lingerie, Facebook is as appealing for what stays hidden as for what is revealed!"
—Danny Devriendt

About Danny Devriendt

A successful blogger and an avid user of social media, Danny is one of the leading authorities on digital media and the predictive web in Europe. He is a European representative in Porter Novelli's Global Digital Council and heads up Porter Novelli's global social media efforts. His base of operations is @PNBR5, a social media lab at the very core of Porter Novelli, Brussels, from where he coordinates PN's cross-border digital activities.

Danny studied Educational Sciences and Agogics, the social science relating to the promotion of personal, social and cultural welfare. His healthy passion for people, Schrödinger's cat, quantum mechanics, and *The Hitchhiker's Guide to the Galaxy* make him an unorthodox, out-of-the-box thinker.

Danny was a journalist for eight years and one of the first Belgian journalists to cover the Internet. His portfolio included several Belgian newspapers and various publications of the Roularta Media Group, as chief-editor for a couple of them. He was a freelancer for the Meridian News service in the United Kingdom and was the cofounder/chief editor of *Le Grand Boulevard*, a stylish monthly news magazine. He also worked for the Belgian National Radio and local television, where he specialized in ICT, lifestyle, and socioeconomic news. He joined Porter Novelli, Brussels, in 1998, heading up the PN Brussels technology division.

A passionate presenter, Danny speaks regularly on the integrated use of digital media, web 3.0, augmented reality, predictive web, crowdsourcing and metrics, and conversation management. He has conducted media and digital media training sessions and seminars for brands and organizations all over the globe. His vision on digital and social media is daily voiced through his Twitter channel @dannydevriendt, his personal blog (heliade.net), and a plethora of online forums.

Expert Answers to Key Social Media Questions

How Has Social Media Benefited Your Business/Personal Brand?

An online brand (personal or other) is measured in *social capital*. This is further defined by your ability/likelihood to connect with influencers and by looking at stats such as your influencer score and credible reach on metrics portals such as PeerIndex.com.

I have found social media the most effective way to build my online brand and to earn my social capital, which has translated itself into my working role and the relationships I am able to build and sustain with potential clients.

> Remember that your online brand is measured in Social Capital.

How and Why Do You Use Twitter?

I use Twitter mainly to connect to other people. It is a great channel that enables me to reach out and virtually touch others in a multitude of countries, regions, and sociographic levels. My *twitterville* brings me refreshing ideas, fascinating content and provides daily food for thought.

I try to push one-third of content myself through Twitter, I retweet/forward one-third of valuable content found by others, and aim to keep one-third of my tweets for personal conversations. For me, it's a search/spread/connect/converse tool.

> My twitterville brings me refreshing ideas, content and provides daily food for thought.

Do You Think Using Your Real Name (or Surname) in Your Twitter ID (or Any Other Profile ID) Is Good or Is Using Your Company/Brand Name Better?

For me, Twitter is a personal thing, so I tweet using my own name, *under* my own name. For brands, tweeting under their brand names can make sense, but they should add the name of the "human" tweep somewhere, ideally in the profile (like "Nikita is tweeting for Marcello.ink").

> My Facebook content sketches a good blueprint of the real me, without exhibiting too much.

How and Why Do You Use Facebook?

I use Facebook to connect to friends, colleagues, and family in a "multimedia way." For me, Facebook is one of the channels I use to spread my messages. My content is a mixture of insights into my more private life, spiced up with thoughts from my blog and lots of pictures and video. Facebook sketches a good blueprint of the real me, without exhibiting too much. Like fine lingerie, Facebook is as appealing for what stays hidden as for what is revealed.

Is YouTube Important? Do You Have Advice About Creating Great Video Content?

YouTube is a great hosting/sharing source for video but not more than that. For me, it's the place where I "park" my videos. I spread those videos through my other channels. For creating great content, there are some short rules:

- Your video needs a plot.

- It needs a smile.

- It needs to be perfect without looking overworked.

Do not plan to be viral, but strive to be awesome.

Is LinkedIn Important, and If So, How Do You Use It?

For me, LinkedIn is just another way of replacing my Rolodex. I use it to update my resumé and to see where other people are going. I do not use it to really engage because I have other channels that are way more effective for that.

Do You Have a Blog? If So, What Advice Can You Give to Newbie Bloggers?

When it comes to blogging, you need to make sure that you can drive/find enough content for the long run. Way too many people start enthusiastically and then run out of steam within weeks. Here are my recommendations for a great blog:

- Work with an editorial calendar and change the range of your topics.

- Engage with other bloggers and read *lots* of them.

- Remember, a blog is not about you; it is about reaching and engaging other people.

- Position your blog in the center of your own online ecosystem and aggregate it out on other channels.

- Compelling eye candy helps, but a blog is dependent upon the quality and frequency of good to great content.

- The ability to identify trending topics and comment on those in a way that adds value is a condition *sine qua non* for building a successful blog.

- Do not forget to link to your main sources of inspiration, and do not take the writing too seriously. A little wink, lots of personality, and a whisper of humor should do the trick.

- List your blog where you would like it to be found and spend as much time in finding the right *tags* as on writing the post.

> Way too many people start blogging enthusiastically and then run out of steam within weeks.

How Much Time Do You Spend on Social Media Activities Each Day, and How Important Do You Think Social Media Time Management Is?

Social media is a big part of my life and my work, so I spent several hours a day. Time management is important and needs to be calibrated on the following: Does what you do add value to your personal social capital or to your clients' benefit? If not, scale down. It is easy to be "grabbed by the fire hose," so constant monitoring is necessary to avoid wasting time. Don't spend *any* time promoting yourself if your content isn't good; others will do that for you. Epitaphs are *earned*, not claimed.

Danny's Top Tips for Social Media Success

- Be yourself.

- Engage daily.

- Provide great content.

- Be respectful and learn from others as much as you teach.

- Be humble but stand by your viewpoints.

- Build an ecosystem of platforms rather than focusing on one channel.

Index

W

W3Counter, 155

widgets
 moving, 83
 overview, 82-83
 plugins compared, 81
 selecting, 82

Widgets directory
 (WordPress), 82-83

Winfrey, Oprah, 10

word count limits, determining, 68

WordPress
 described, 69
 Widgets directory, 82-83

WordTracker, 129

Y

Yahoo! Answers, documenting
responses to relevant questions on, 74

Yelp, 61

YouTube
 audience, connection to, 53
 authenticity in videos, 53
 blogs
  *answering how-to ques-
   tion related to your
   business, 74*
  embedding video, 88-90
 brand, deciding on user-
  name to represent your,
  45
 case studies shown on, 45
 channel customization
  *background image,
   adding, 50-51*
  *modules, managing,
   51-52*
  settings for, 47-48
  steps for, 47-52
  *theme, selecting channel,
   49-50*
 customer testimonials, 45
 described, 44
 distribution of videos, 53

expert in field, marking
 yourself as, 53
feedback comments
 through, 44
first YouTube video, 52-53
global audience for local
 event with, 44
guidelines for, 53
history of, 44
incentives for viewers to
 upload videos about your
 products and services,
 creating, 53
length of videos for, 53
product reviews, 45
question-and-answer
 videos, 53
signing up for, 45-46
simplicity in videos, prefer-
 ence for, 53
slide shows and demon-
 strations used as your
 first YouTube video, existing company, 52-53
use of
 Danny Devriendt, 192
 Jeff Bullas, 166
 Jessica Northey, 184-185
 Lori McNee, 173
 Paul Steele, 178
username for, 45-46
uses for, 44-45
video tutorials on, 44
video-editing software,
 using, 52
videos and playlists, customizing your display of,
 54

Z

Zuckerberg, Mark, 11, 29-30
"The Zuckerberg Revolution"
 (Gabler), 11

SOCIAL LOCATION MARKETING
Outshining Your Competitors on Foursquare, Gowalla, Yelp & Other Location Sharing Sites

SOCIAL MEDIA ROI
Managing and Measuring Social Media Efforts in Your Organization
OLIVIER BLANCHARD

BLOGGING TO DRIVE BUSINESS
Create and Maintain Valuable Customer Connections
ERIC BUTOW & REBECCA BOLLWITT

FACEBOOK MARKETING
THIRD EDITION
Designing Your Next Marketing Campaign
JUSTIN R. LEVY

MAKE THE MOST OF YOUR SMARTPHONE, TABLET, COMPUTER, AND MORE! CHECK OUT THE MY…BOOK SERIES

Full-Color, Step-by-Step Guides

The "My…" series is a visually rich, task-based series to help you get up and running with your new device and technology, and tap into some of the hidden, or less obvious, features. The organized, task-based format allows you to quickly and easily find exactly the task you want to accomplish, and then shows you how to achieve it with minimal text and plenty of visual cues.

Visit quepublishing.com/mybooks to learn more about the My… book series from Que.

quepublishing.com

FREE Online Edition

Your purchase of **Zero to 100,000** includes access to a free online edition for 45 days through the Safari Books Online subscription service. Nearly every Que book is available online through Safari Books Online, along with more than 5,000 other technical books and videos from publishers such as Addison-Wesley Professional, Cisco Press, Exam Cram, IBM Press, O'Reilly, Prentice Hall, and Sams.

SAFARI BOOKS ONLINE allows you to search for a specific answer, cut and paste code, download chapters, and stay current with emerging technologies.

Activate your FREE Online Edition at
www.informit.com/safarifree

> **STEP 1:** Enter the coupon code: MOHMPEH.

> **STEP 2:** New Safari users, complete the brief registration form. Safari subscribers, just log in.

If you have difficulty registering on Safari or accessing the online edition, please e-mail customer-service@safaribooksonline.com